THE GREAT INVERTED PYRAMID

THE GREAT INVERTED PYRAMID

What Is Money and How Do We Count It?

Sam J. Dealey

To order additional copies of this book, contact:
Xlibris Corporation
1-888-795-4274
www.Xlibris.com
Orders@Xlibris.com
66835

To Redford, Roach, Lieb and Gordon

CONTENTS

INTRODUCTION

This little primer on monetary history in the United States in the last two centuries is a self-study guide directed to intelligent citizens who want a quick read and lots of references where they can find out more.

Two questions recur throughout this study: "What's money?" and "How do we count it?" Beaver pelts have intrinsic worth, serve as a medium of exchange in the short run, and are a repository of value in a longer time frame. You can do business with them; they are finite, tangible and countable. They are a commodity currency as is gold, silver, nylon stockings, and cigarettes. The dollar bill in my pocket is something else. I can do business with it as well, but it is only the government's promise that it will remain a stable unit of account and that I can use it as a medium of exchange now and in the future. It is a fiduciary or 'fiat' currency. But I don't even carry around many dollar bills; an encoded plastic card connects me electronically with my intergalactic credits, and a machine in the wall in London or Paris will give me pounds or euros at my pleasure. I can cash a certificate of deposit, sign a note at my bank, or call my broker and sell stock, wire money to Hong Kong, and the Chinese government can buy US treasury securities in New York. Neither gold nor paper went anywhere; electronic blips flew around the world in less than a moment. Where's the money? Was it stock, a CD, a bank loan, a wire transfer, the treasury bonds? A page of history is, indeed, worth more than a book of theory. The Panic of 2007 is really not much different from the Panic of 1907. The bubble got too big.

Short chapters are followed by the most valuable references, some modern and some pretty old. A complete source of citations and references is in the Annotated Chronology. The following books are fundamental, as appropriate, for the entire study. Friedman & Schwartz is still the classic for post-Civil War history, but Timberlake is far easier to read as history.

Dewey, Davis Rich, *Financial History of the United States* (Longmans, Green, 1903); reprinted 2007.
Dunne, Gerald T., *Monetary Decisions of the Supreme Court* (Rutgers, 1960).
Milton Friedman & Anna J. Schwartz, *A Monetary History of the United States, 1867-1960* (Princeton Univ. Press, 1963).

Bray Hammond, *Banks and Politics in America from the Revolution to the Civil War* (Princeton Univ. Press, 1957).

Alonzo B. Hepburn, *A History of Currency in the United States* (Macmillan, 1903, rev. ed. 1915).

Allan H. Meltzer, *A History of the Federal Reserve System*, 2 vols. (Univ. Chic. Press, 2003 & est. 2009)

Timberlake, Richard H., *Monetary Policy in the United States: An Intellectual and Institutional History* (Univ. Chic. Press, 1993)

Wicker, Elmus: Professor Wicker has published several excellent short works on financial panics and the early Federal Reserve. See chapter citations.

Note on Grains and Ounces

An ounce can be avoirdupois, troy or fluid. You weigh yourself in avoirdupois pounds which have sixteen ounces, and this ounce is 437.5 grains, or 28.349 grams. Gold and silver, however, are measured in troy ounces, 480 grains, 31.103 grams.

A silver dollar weighs 412.5 grains of alloyed silver (ninety percent fine) and contains 371.25 grains of fine (pure) silver. Thus an ounce of silver (since 1837) was worth at the mint $1.2929 per fine troy ounce (FTO) or 480 divided by 371.25.

A twenty-dollar gold piece weighs 516 grains of alloyed gold (ninety percent fine) and contains 464.4 grains fine gold. Thus gold, from 1834 to 1934, was valued at $20.67 per FTO, or 480 divided by 464.4 times 20. So the established ratio in value by law was 16 to 1, the source of endless trouble.

Note on Supreme Court Cases

Sovereignty and federalism in monetary affairs have been in the courts from the earliest days. Here are some cases, not discussed in the text, which are full of history. Read them at your leisure.

Bank of the United States:

> McCulloch v. Maryland, 4 Wheat. (17 US) 316 (1819)
> Osborn v. Bank of the United States, 9 Wheat. (22 US) 738 (1824)

State Bank Note Cases:

> Briscoe v. Bank of Kentucky, 11 Pet. (36 US) 257 (1837)
> Veazie Bank v. Fenno, 8 Wall (75 US) 533 (1869)

The Legal Tender Cases:

> Hepburn v. Griswold, 8 Wall. (75 US) 603 (1870)
> Knox v. Lee, 12 Wall. (79 US) 457 (1871)
> Julliard v. Greenman, 110 US 421 (1884)

The Gold Clause Cases:

> Nortz v. United States, 294 U.S. 317 (1935)
> Perry v. United States, 294 U.S. 330 (1935)

CHAPTER ONE

THE COLONIAL EXPERIENCE
AND THE NEW NATION

In colonial days money was scarce, and what passed as money was varied. Beaver skins, wampum, musket balls and tobacco were all used as money. Foreign coins were common; only a few American colonies briefly minted coinage. The eight reale silver coins minted in Spain and in Spanish colonies, generally called a 'Spanish milled dollar', was probably most popular and widely used. It could be cut into eight bits for subsidiary coinage and thus the nickname 'two bits' for a quarter. The reale coin was about 385 troy grains of fine silver. Although Parliament attempted to define the rates of exchange for foreign coins, each colony set its own standard.

The first issue of currency in America was by Massachusetts in 1690 to pay for an expedition against Canada. The colonies issued lots of bills of credit denominated in coinage but generally unredeemable in coin, although some were actually sunk or redeemed in real money. The colonies did not shirk from imposing these bills on the community by legal penalties. These bills could be issued upon the credit of the colony as a promise to pay, or at least to be received for taxes, or upon mortgage of land, much as the assignat issuance in France. The issuance of paper money started as a little colonial fever and ended in an inflationary plague requiring action of Parliament to stop it. Currency Acts of 1751 and 1764, applying first to the greatest offenders and finally to all the colonies, prohibited colonies from issuing paper bills and making them legal tender. This problem, and the experience of the Revolution, led to our constitutional prohibition on states issuing bills of credit.

The colonial experience sets the stage for discussion of money. There are three generally acknowledged characteristics of money which remain live policy issues today.

First that it serves as a medium of exchange and passes in the market as a means of current payment
Second that it serves as a unit of account.
Third that it be a repository of value over time.

This third characteristic has been the great failing of all soft money schemes. They depreciate.

Commencement of the American Revolution brought forth an assortment of currencies. The best estimates of specie in all the colonies were eight to ten million dollars. The colonies all issued paper money and the first monetary business of the Second Continental Congress, which met from May 10, 1775, until ratification of the Articles of Confederation on March 1, 1781, was the authorization and issuance of bills of credit; but since the Congress couldn't tax, it had lots of bills and not much credit. Congress issued some $240,000,000 in Continental Bills of Credit between 1775 and 1780.These bills of credit pledged repayment in Spanish-milled dollars but began to depreciate toward the end of 1777; by 1779 the depreciation was rampant enough that Congress pledged on September 1, 1779, not to emit more than two hundred million dollars of bills of credit (14 JCC 1013).

Congress recognized by early 1780 that some sort of currency reform was necessary. On March 18, 1780, it determined to retire the existing currency (called 'Old Tenor' bills) by having the colonies collect enough of the currency or pay in specie, at a rate of forty-to-one, to retire $15,000,000 per month. (16 JCC 260) Congress would then issue new bills of credit ('New Tenor' bills) at a rate of one for each twenty old tenor bills destroyed. These new tenor bills also quickly sank in value.

A summary of emissions of continental currency is presented in a note; many of these issues were supplemental to previous printings so there are many fewer dates on actual currency than these authorizations. The Assumption Act of August 4, 1790, finally proposed to pay off these bills at a ratio of one hundred to one. Authorities in each colony printed money as well; Virginia was probably the biggest offender.

From March 18, 1780, Congress financed the war by hand-to-mouth begging from the colonies and borrowing abroad. The report of a special committee on April 18, 1781, at 19 JCC 402, is a particularly useful summary of just how bad it was. Congress did come to realize the relationship between money-supply and inflation; but since they couldn't tax, what else could they do but print and borrow. The currency issued by each colony was generally as bad as that issued by Congress. It wasn't worth a Continental, but was enforced by severe legal tender laws in each colony. The figures are uncertain. The Board of Treasury in 1786 reported that $241,562,775 of old tenor bills had been issued and $111,406,124 destroyed in the currency reform (30 JCC 22); other writers have made different calculations.

A good bit of time under the Articles of Confederation (1781-1789) was spent discussing money. Robert Morris, Thomas Jefferson, and the Grand Committee all issued reports, and the Congress determined the weight of coinage and authorized but did not establish a mint. The Constitutional Convention met May 25, 1787, and completed the Constitution September 17, 1787; it was ratified by the requisite nine states June 21, 1788 and during the months following first meeting on the Congress on March 4, 1789, the government was slowly established. Passage of the Tariff Act of July 4, 1789, was a high priority; for nine years the government of the United States had lived on borrowings abroad and begging at home from the states; on August 4, 1790, the Assumption Act was passed to provide for consolidation of the national and colonial debts. Hamilton presented his Report on a Mint (January 28, 1791), and finally in 1792 the Congress established a mint and the weight of coins.

Banks were rare and viewed with considerable trepidation. They were a source of both currency and disaster. The Bank of North America was incorporated in 1781; the Bank of New York, Bank of Massachusetts, and Bank of Pennsylvania were the only state banks.

Realizing, nevertheless, that a bank might act as a repository of funds and aid in financing government operations, Congress, on February 25, 1791, established The President, Directors and Company, of the Bank of the United States with a twenty-year charter and a capital of $10,000,000 of which the government would subscribe for one-fifth. The bank opened in Philadelphia with branches ultimately in New York, Boston, Baltimore, Washington, Norfolk, Charleston, Savannah and New Orleans. The bank was not re-chartered in 1811 on the grounds of unconstitutionality and, more probably, on the grounds of political animosity.

From the earliest time the question was whether a bank needed to keep all the specie deposited in exchange for an equal amount of its circulating bank notes and deposits (100% reserve banking) or could issue circulating notes in exchange for customer's promissory notes in some multiple of specie deposits, keeping only enough specie on hand to redeem its circulating notes presented for redemption across the counter (fractional reserve banking). A national currency (bills of exchange issued by the government) was thought to be unconstitutional as well as unwise.

Americans could watch while the French Revolution and Napoleonic Wars presented the finest examples of ruinous national monetary creation. Specie, of course, disappeared from general circulation. In France, government had lots of property, mostly confiscated church and royalist lands. What better plan than to issue a currency redeemable in land? That couldn't be worthless; the domaines nationaux could be monetized and the want of currency satisfied. The first issue of assignats was 400,000,000 livres in April, 1790; by 1796 the total emission was around 45,000,000,000. From the beginning it rapidly became rather useless although acceptance was enforced by draconian legal provisions. The assignats were replaced by mandats at a ratio of 30 to 1, but they also quickly fell to 3% of face value. Finally, in 1797, the printing plates were destroyed, and France reverted to barter, specie, and foreign coin. The patriots, who had parted with something, ended up with nothing.

In England, things were a little better. From 1797 until 1821, banknotes were unconvertible but could be traded for specie. A Parliamentary Select Committee on the High Price of Gold Bullion intelligently studied and reported June 8, 1810 (the Bullion Report) that the high price of bullion was probably due to an excessive quantity of banknotes.

Note on Issues of Old Tenor Continental Currency

22 Jun 75	$ 2,000,000	2 JCC 103
25 Jul 75	$ 1,000,000	2 JCC 207
29 Nov 75	$ 3,000,000	3 JCC 390
5 Jan 76	$ 10,000	4 JCC 32
17 Feb 76	$ 4,000,000	4 JCC 157
9 May 76	$ 5,000,000	4 JCC 339
22 Jul 76	$ 5,000,000	5 JCC 599
2 Nov 76	$ 500,000	6 JCC 818
28 Dec 76	$ 5,000,000	6 JCC 1047
26 Feb 77	$ 5,000,000	7 JCC 161
20 May 77	$ 5,000,000	7 JCC 373
15 Aug 77	$ 1,000,000	8 JCC 646
7 Nov 77	$ 1,000,000	9 JCC 873
3 Dec 77	$ 1,000,000	9 JCC 993
8 Jan 78	$ 1,000,000	10 JCC 28
22 Jan 78	$ 2,000,000	10 JCC 82
16 Feb 78	$ 2,000,000	10 JCC 174
5 Mar 78	$ 2,000,000	10 JCC 223
4 Apr 78	$ 1,000,000	10 JCC 309
11 Apr 78	$ 5,000,000	10 JCC 337
18 Apr 78	$ 500,000	10 JCC 365
22 May 78	$ 5,000,000	11 JCC 524
20 Jun 78	$ 5,000,000	11 JCC 627
31 Jul 78	$ 5,000,000	11 JCC 731
5 Sep 78	$ 5,000,000	12 JCC 884
26 Sep 78	$ 10,000,000	12 JCC 962
4 Nov 78	$ 10,000,000	12 JCC 1100
14 Dec 78	$ 10,000,000	12 JCC 1218
14 Jan 79	$ 50,000,400	13 JCC 64

3 Feb 79	$ 5,000,160	13 JCC 139
19 Feb 79	$ 5,000,160	13 JCC 209
1 Apr 79	$ 5,000,160	13 JCC 408
5 May 79	$ 10,000,100	14 JCC 548
4 Jun 79	$ 10,000,100	14 JCC 687
17 Jul 79	$ 5,000,180	14 JCC 848
17 Jul 79	$ 10,000,100	14 JCC 848
17 Sep 79	$ 5,000,000	15 JCC 1076
17 Sep 79	$ 10,000,080	15 JCC1076
14 Oct 79	$ 5,000,180	15 JCC 1171
17 Nov 79	$ 5,000,040	15 JCC 1285
17 Nov 79	$ 5,000,500	15 JCC 1285
29 Nov 79	$ 10,000,140	15 JCC 1324

The collections of currency at Notre Dame, *www.coins.nd.edu/ColCurrency*, and the Brock Center at the University of Virginia, *http://etext.virginia.edu/users/brock*, are noteworthy.

NOTE ON THE CIRCULATION OF FOREIGN COIN IN THE UNITED STATES

Foreign coins have always circulated in America and were legal tender until 1857. A Proclamation dated June 18, 1705, and The Act for ascertaining the Rates of Foreign Coins, 6 Anne c.30 (1709) attempted to set exchange rates for Spanish dollars as well as other foreign coins. The colonies separately tried to establish rates of exchange. See Laws of Virginia, October 1710, ch. X; November 1714, ch. I; and February 1727, ch. IX, 4 Henning's Statutes 218-220.

Congress passed the Act regulating foreign coins, 2d Cong., Sess. II, ch. 5, 1 Stat. 300 (February 9, 1793), which set rates at which foreign coins could pass a legal tender. This statute was extended in various forms:

Act regulating the currency of foreign coins, 9th Cong., Sess. I, ch. 22, 2 Stat.374 (April 10, 1806)

Act regulating the value of certain foreign coins, 23d Cong., Sess. I, ch. 96, 4 Stat 700 (June 28, 1834)

Act regulating the currency of foreign gold and silver coins, 27th Cong., Sess. III, ch.69, 5 Stat. 607 (March 3, 1843)

Act relating to Foreign Coins, 34th Cong., Sess. III, ch. 56, 11 Stat 163 (February 21, 1857)

References for Chapter One

Brock, Leslie V., *The Currency of the American Colonies, 1700-1764: A Study in Colonial Finance and Imperial Relations* (New York, 1975) This is rare and expensive; try a university library.

Brock, Leslie V., *The Colonial Currency, Prices, and Exchange Rates*, 34 Essays in History, Univ. of Virginia (1992)

Chernow, Ron, *Alexander Hamilton* (Penguin, New York, 2004) Only chapter 18 deals with money, banks and mints.

Dewey, Davis Rich, *Financial History of the United States* (Longman, Green, 1903)

Edling, Max M., *So immense a power in the affairs of war:Alexander Hamilton and the Restoration of Public Credit*, 64 Wm & Mary Quarterly 237-326 (2007)

Ernst, Joseph Albert, *Money and Politics in America, 1755-1775* (Univ. NC, 1973)

Ferguson, E. James, *The Power of the Purse: A History of American Public Finance, 1776-1790* (UNC, 1961)

Hamilton, Alexander, *Report on the Establishment of a Mint* in Syrett, Harold C., Ed., *Papers of Alexander Hamilton* (Columbia, Vol. VII, 1963) at 570-607

Hamilton, Alexander, *Report on a National Bank* in Syrett, Harold C., Ed., *Papers of Alexander Hamilton* (Columbia, Vol. VII, 1963) at 305-342

Holdsworth, John T., and Dewey, Davis R., *The First and Second Banks of the United States* (National Monetary Commission, 61st Cong., 2d Sess, Sen Doc 571 (1910)

Jefferson, Thomas, *Notes on Coinage* in Boyd, Julian P., Ed., *Papers of Thomas Jefferson* (Princeton, Vol 7, 1953) at150-185

Miller, John C., *Triumph of Freedom, 1775-1783* (Little, Brown, 1948) See the chapter Inflation and Its Consequences (pages 425-477).

McCusker, John J., *Money and Exchange in Europe in America, 1600-1775* (Univ. NC, 1978).

McCusker, John J., & Menard, Russell, *The Economy of British American, 1607-1789* (Chapel Hill, 1985)

McDonald, Forrest, *Alexander Hamilton* (1979). Read this; it is a vastly better treatment of Hamilton's economic thought than Chernow.

Morris, Robert, *Report* in Ferguson, E. James, Ed., *Papers of Robert Morris* (Pittsburg, Vol 4, 1978) at 30-38

Newman, Eric P., *The Early Paper Money of America: Colonial Currency 1696-1810* (1967).

Priest, Claire, *Currency Policies and Legal Development in Colonial New England*, 110 Yale L. J. 1303-1405 (2001)

Sumner, William Graham, *The Financier and the Finances of the American Revolution* (1891)

Sumner, William Graham, *A History of American Currency* (1874) (Reprint, Augustus M. Kelley, 1968)

Wright, Robert E., and Cowen, David J., *Financial Founding Fathers* (Univ. Chic. 2006)

White, Andrew Dickson, *Fiat Money Inflation in France* (1876), which is widely reprinted.

Chapter Two

New Nation, Bank War and Independent Treasury

The 1790s actually worked pretty well in contrast to the 1780s. The national debt stayed about the same, but tariff revenues did meet current expenses. Despite blockades and embargoes, the decade of 1800 to 1810 was good; the revenues exceeded expenses and the national debt was reduced.

The War of 1812 brought significant financial strains. The United States were militarily and financially unprepared. Customs receipts fell off dramatically because of the maritime war, so Congress issued, over the two year period, some $37,000,000 in bonds, but mindful of the history of the continental currency, did not attempt to make these legal tender issues. The currency doubled, and state banking institutions tripled in number between 1811 and 1816.

Secretary of the Treasury Dallas proposed a new national bank in 1814 and, after extended debate, Congress repented and created a second corporation and body politic, by the name and style of "the president, directors, and company, of the bank of the United States". This entity had a capital of $35,000,000, of which the government took one-fifth. The first two years after opening in 1817 were marked by a post-war slump, bad weather, and collapse of money; the federal budget, however, quickly regained a surplus and the bank quickly became successful in issuing sound bank notes.

The charter of the Second Bank of the United States by law was for twenty years from its creation in 1816, but political discussion of renewal of the charter began as early as 1829. A number of differing but overlapping interests inhabited the political landscape. There were those who had constitutional objections to the existence of a national bank, those who believed in hard money, those who believed in state banking, those who favored an early brand of loose money populism, those who recognized the usefulness of a national bank, and those who favored an independent sub-treasury system. The mix was heated by intense animosity between Andrew Jackson and Nicholas Biddle, President of the Bank of the United States. This was an age of political greats; the history is fabulous but too involved to relate at length. Like the Great Depression, this era is still widely debated.

A thoroughly debated bill to extend the charter of the bank passed the Congress in early July, 1832; but on July 10, the President vetoed it ostensibly on the basis of monopoly and unconstitutionality, and the bank became a major issue in the 1832 campaign. In the early fall of 1833, Jackson and his Attorney-General, Roger Taney, struck at the bank. Jackson informed the cabinet that government deposits would be removed from the bank; the Secretary of the Treasury, Duane, refused and was fired; Taney was named Secretary and issued orders on September 26 to remove federal deposits and place them in state banks. This produced a new uproar in the Senate; Taney's reasons for withdrawing the deposits were deemed unsatisfactory and insufficient and Jackson was declared to have assumed authority in derogation of the constitution and laws. So in the spring of 1834, the Senate censured the President, and the President censured the Senate. Thus it stood. After expiration of the bank's charter there were no more national banks until 1863.

Considerable speculation in the purchase of public lands in 1835 and early 1836, mostly for state bank notes, led to issuance of the Specie Circular on July 11, 1836, by Secretary of the Treasury Levi Woodbury. Receivers of public money and deposit banks were directed to take nothing but gold and silver in payment for public lands. This was the law but apparently had been largely ignored in the West. In the usual florid language of the times the object was stated to be to "withhold any countenance . . . from the monopoly of the public lands in the hands of speculators and capitalists . . . and to discourage the ruinous extension of bank issues, and bank credits . . ."

Whether due to the Specie Circular, the Deposit Act of June 23, 1836 [Can you believe it? A federal surplus of some $28,000,000 was distributed to the states in 1837], or import-export problems, a serious specie drain and banking panic occurred in 1837 and recession continued for several more years. Van Buren didn't have a clue or an answer.

To his credit Jackson had proposed that a new, different, and improved Bank of the United States be established; nothing was done until passage of the first Independent Treasury Act on July 4, 1840. The Whig election of 1840 produced profound changes. The hero of Tippecanoe, William Henry Harrison, and John Tyler, too, were elected, and both houses of Congress had Whig majorities. A month later Harrison died and Tyler became President. Henry Clay, leader in the Senate, produced a repeal of the Independent Treasury on August 13, 1841, and moved on to propose a Fiscal Bank of the United States. It passed and Tyler vetoed it August 16, 1841; Clay passed a second Fiscal Corporation bill and Tyler vetoed it also on September 9, 1841. Finally a second Independent Treasury Act was passed August 6, 1846. The sub-treasury system continued until 1920.

———

During this period after expiration of the second Bank of the United States, all banks were state banks until 1863. Their assets consisted of specie and notes from customers; their liabilities consisted of deposits and their own circulating banknotes. Regulation differed between the states. Some banks failed, some succeeded, but the country went forward. Hugh McCulloch's description of the State Bank of Indiana shows how it could and should be done.

References for Chapter Two

Bowers, Claude G., *The Party Battles of the Jackson Period* (Houghton Mifflin, 1928)

Catterall, Ralph C. H., *The Second Bank of the United States* (Univ. Chic. 1903)

Dwyer, Gerald P., Jr., *Wildcat Banking, Banking Panics, and Free Banking in the United States*, Federal Reserve Bank, Atlanta, Economic Review (December, 1996)

Gallatin, Albert, *Selected Writings of Albert Gallatin* (E. James Ferguson, ed.), (Bobbs-Merrill, 1967). See particularly Gallatin's *Considerations on the Currency and Banking System of the United States* in *Writings of Albert Gallatin*, ed. Henry Adams, Vol. III, pages 233-364, and *Suggestions on the Banks and Currency of the Several United States*, Vol. III, pages 365-488 (Antiquarian Press reprint, 1960).

Holdsworth, John Thom & Dewey, Davis R., *The First and Second Banks of the United States* (61st Cong., 2d Sess, Sen Doc 571, 1910) National Monetary Commission

Holt, Michael F., *The Rise and Fall of the American Whig Party* (Oxford, 1999). This is a compendium of absolutely everything about the Whig party. To loosely quote Forrest McDonald, Mr. Holt looked at the forest and described the leaves.

Kinley, David, *The History, Organization and Influence of the Independent Treasury of the United States* (Crowell, 1893).

Knox, John Jay, *A History of Banking in the United States* (1903) (Reprint, Augustus M. Kelley, 1969) The *Specie Circular* is at pp. 81-82.

Peterson, Merrill D., *The Great Triumvirate: Webster, Clay, and Calhoun* (Oxford, 1987)

Remini, Robert, *Andrew Jackson and the Bank War* (Norton, 1967)

Remini, Robert, *Henry Clay: Statesman for the Union* (Norton, 1991)

Rousseau, Peter L., *Jacksonian Monetary Policy, Specie Flows, and the Panic of 1837* (Vanderbilt WP 00-W04R, 2001)

Wise, Henry A., *Seven Decades of the Union* (Lippincott, 1872) John Tyler's side of the story.

CHAPTER THREE

CIVIL WAR AND GREENBACKS

The Civil War turned out to last longer and to cost more, in every way, than was generally expected. The changes in national banking practice and in finance of the government were profound. Seventy-five thousand volunteers for ninety day enlistments didn't half do it.

At the beginning of the war the currency consisted of about $250,000,000 in specie and some $200,000,000 of state bank notes; by the end of the war, there was practically no circulating specie, some state bank notes, a new national bank note issued by national banks, interest-legal tender treasury notes, and non-interest-bearing legal tender United States Notes called 'greenbacks'.

As always, war finance was paramount. Lincoln appointed Salmon Portland Chase of Ohio as Secretary of the Treasury. There wasn't much in the Treasury, but residual borrowing authority permitted funding at heavy discounts and delay of a major finance bill until the special session of the 37th Congress scheduled for July 4, 1861. Chase's financing proposal was approved July 17, 1861, and authorized borrowing $250,000,000 in a combination of twenty-year 7% bonds, three-year 7.3% notes, or one-year 3.65% notes, with various exchange provisions. A supplemental funding act approved August 5, 1861, permitted refunding the 7.3% notes with twenty-year 6% bonds, and another supplemental act permitting issuance of demand notes was approved February 12, 1862.

Neither American nor international bankers were terribly excited about buying national debt, and reluctantly Chase determined to issue legal tender notes ultimately called 'greenbacks'. The greenback era began with the Legal Tender Act of February 25, 1862, when Congress authorized the issuance of $150,000,000 of United States Notes as legal tender; subsequent acts of July 11, 1862, and March 3, 1863, authorized a total of $400,000,000. After various redemptions and re-issuances, the final amount was fixed by the Banking Act of June 20, 1874, at $382,000,000. The figure generally given as outstanding after the war is around $356,000,000.

National banking began with passage of the National Currency Act on February 25, 1863, supplemented by the National Bank Act on June 3, 1864.

(The second Act is mostly a rearrangement of the first.) Hugh McCulloch, an experienced and distinguished banker from Indiana, became the first Comptroller of the Currency. Unquestionably there was a need for a national currency, but the requirements of the acts also served as a vehicle for the sale and placement of government bonds. The Comptroller of the Currency was authorized to issue up to $300,000,000 of circulating notes to national banks, upon their deposit of United States bonds with the Treasurer. Each bank could receive notes equal to ninety percent of the value of its deposited bonds. To support the circulation of the new national bank currency a corollary action had to be suppression of circulating state bank notes. Section six of the Internal Revenue Act of March 3, 1865, imposed a 10% tax on the banknotes of state banks; this tax was further implemented by an Act of July 13, 1866.

Chase's political machinations in Ohio and in the 1864 elections led to his replacement as secretary by William Pitt Fessenden of Maine on July 5, 1864, who was replaced by Hugh McCulloch on March 9, 1865.

Total debt of the United States in August, 1865, was $2,845,900,000 compared with a beginning balance of $76,000,000. Surprisingly the debt was reduced substantially and relatively quickly. At the close of the war, the national currency consisted in large part of legal tender notes trading at a significant discount to gold. The Specie Resumption Act of 1875 provided a four year window for the Treasury to acquire enough gold to resume redemption of legal tender notes on January 1, 1879. A redeemable note, however, is not necessarily redeemed; legal tender notes remained in circulation for many years. Once they could be redeemed, few people really wanted to redeem them; paper didn't wear holes in their pockets. Greenbacks were permanently fixed at a quantity of $346,681,016 in 1878 and were carried on the Treasury accounts for over a century.

Consider, for a moment, how banks can intermediate government debt. The 'greenback' is straightforward government paper. The government pays it out and says it is money. Alternatively, the government can sell bonds to banks (bank assets) and authorize the banks to issue banknotes (bank liabilities) on the basis of their government bonds. Today the pattern isn't much different: the government issues bonds held by the Fed which issues money held by the people.

Note on Legal Tender and Loan Acts

FEB 25, 1862	12 Stat.345 First Legal Tender Act	$150,000,000
JUL 11, 1862	12 Stat.532 Second Legal Tender Act	$150,000,000
JAN 17, 1863	12 Stat. 822 Joint Res. 9	$100,000,000
MAR 3, 1863	12 Stat. 709 Third Legal Tender Act	$150,000,000 (incl JR 9)
SEP 13,1982	31 USC 5115 US Currency Notes	$300,000,000
JUL 17, 1861	First Loan Act	12 Stat 259
AUG 5, 1861	First Supp Loan Act	12 Stat 313
FEB 12, 1862	Second Supp Loan Act	12 Stat 338
MAR 3, 1863	Third Loan & Third Legal Tender Act	12 Stat 709
MAR 3, 1864	Fourth Loan Act	13 Stat 13
JUN 30, 1864	Fifth Loan Act	13 Stat 218
JAN 28, 1865	Fifth Supp Loan Act	13 Stat 425
MAR 3, 1865	Sixth Loan Act	13 Stat 468

References for Chapter Three

Knox, John Jay, *United States Notes: A History of the Various Issues of Paper Money by the Government of the United States* (Unwin, London, 1885)

Mitchell, Wesley C., *A History of the Greenbacks* (Chicago, 1903)

McCulloch, Hugh, *Men and Measures of Half a Century* (Scribner, New York, 1888)

Niven, John, *Salmon P. Chase* (Oxford, 1995). Good background but not much on money.

Noyes, Alexander Dana, *History of the National Bank Currency* (61st Cong, 2d Sess., Sen Doc 572, 1910) (National Monetary Commission)

Noyes, Alexander Dana, *Forty Years of American Finance* (Putnam, 1909)

Sumner, William Graham, *A History of American Currency* (1874) (Reprint, Augustus M. Kelley, 1968)

Unger, Irwin, *The Greenback Era: A Social and Political History of American Finance* (Princeton, 1964)

Hammond, Bray, *Sovereignty and an Empty Purse* (Princeton, 1970)

Sexton, Jay, *Debtor Diplomacy: Finance and American Foreign Relations in the Civil War Era, 1837-1873* (Oxford, 2005) offers some background on the ups-and-downs of international finance.

CHAPTER FOUR

GOLD AND SILVER—
A DIVERSION ON BIMETALLISM

Bimetallism, the simultaneous circulation of both silver and gold coinage, was always a problem but became a raging issue after the Civil War when the ratio of value departed substantially from the range of 15 or 16 to 1. The value of coinage became a matter of class and regional politics rather than of economics.

Bimetallism can work if the government merely certifies the weight of the coin and its purity or if it limits the cheaper metal to subsidiary coinage. The failure of bimetallism was caused by the attempt to generally legislate the ratio at which the two different metals would circulate. The difficulty of fixed ratio bimetallism was well known to the founding fathers.

Robert Morris, the Financier, in his Report dated January 15, 1782, discussed the effect of trading between a fifteen to one ratio established in England and a fourteen to one ratio established in France and concludes that it must follow that in a short time all the gold coins of full weight would be in England; and all the silver coins of full weight in France. Similarly Thomas Jefferson in his *Notes on Coinage*, written between March and May, 1784, calls the proportion between the values of gold and silver a mercantile problem altogether, and notes that the legal proportion in Spain is 16 for 1, in England 15.5 for 1 and in France 15 for 1. The Spaniards and English are found in experience to retain an over-proportion of gold coins and lose their silver. The French have a greater proportion of silver.

The most thorough discussion of the relative proportions and values of silver and gold coinage are presented by Alexander Hamilton in his January 28, 1791, *Report on the Establishment of a Mint*. Hamilton discusses the effect of mis-valuing the ratio of gold and silver coins; that one or the other will suffer banishment, but nevertheless concludes that 15 to 1 will probably be found the most eligible.

Although the issues of weight and fineness of coinage had been discussed by Morris, Jefferson, and Hamilton, nothing actually effectual passed the Congress until April 2, 1792. In spite of knowledge of the difficulties of bimetallism at a fixed ratio, it was adopted, apparently in the conviction that the country needed a monetary unit and a national coinage other than a measure by weight of one metal or the other at a specified standard or even the circulation of foreign coinage. This turned out not to be so. Hamilton suggested that the foreign gold coins be given currency for a maximum of three years, but they, in fact, continued to have legal status until 1857. It is astounding that fixed ratio bimetallism could last so long and cause so much trouble. The problem was known as Gresham's Law. Bad money (the over-valued money) drives good money (the under-valued money) out of circulation. The history of legal bimetallism is the story of the changing market rates for precious metals.

1792 to 1834: In 1792 Congress established a ratio of 15 (silver) to 1 (gold) which was close at that time to the commercial ratio. Production of silver was increasing, however, and the ratio moved over the next few years to 15.5 to one (France, 1803) and 16 to 1 (England, 1816). Silver was the cheaper metal and was over-valued in the United States. Thus one could pay 15 ounces of silver for 1 ounce of gold in the United States and sell that 1 ounce of gold for 16 ounces of silver in Europe. Gold coinage was hoarded or exported. Most of the coinage in the US consisted of French and Spanish silver.

1834-1874: In 1834 the gold content of the dollar was decreased so that the ratio was 16 to 1. This slightly over-valued gold by about fifty cents per ounce. The ratio did not exceed 16 to 1 until 1873. During this period gold became the practical standard. An ounce of gold was worth 16 ounces of silver in the US and 15.something in Europe. Send silver to Europe and get more gold for your silver than at the US mint.

1874 to 1896: The Silver War. Bimetallism did not begin to heat up as a political issue until the commercial ratio of silver versus gold began to change significantly. A silver boom in the United States began in the late 1850s, particularly with recognition of the Comstock Lode, around 1859. Most silver was exported because the market was more favorable abroad. The Coinage Act of 1873 did not provide for coinage of the standard silver dollar, but did provide smaller silver coins and for silver "trade dollar" of 420 grains troy standard, a heavier coin, compared with 412.5 standard grains per dollar previously set in 1837. This trade dollar coin was intended for export and was discontinued in 1887; it is widely counterfeited today.

Around 1873 the commercial ratio began to change dramatically and the silver interests desperately wanted to sell silver to the government at the price of $1.2929 per troy ounce (sixteen to one). Silver production increased steadily and as the value of silver fell, it took more and more silver to get an ounce of gold. By 1878, the ratio was above 17 to 1 and ten years later was above 22 to 1, but the US official ratio remained 16 to 1. An odd coalition of silver producers, debtors, and greenbackers railed against the imagined "Crime of 73". According to Senator Sherman, all the racket was simply "to secure a cheaper dollar of less purchasing power, with the view to enable debtors to pay debts, contracted on the basis of gold coin, with silver coins, worth, with free coinage, less than one-half of gold coin." The issue may have been more complicated since economic growth exceeded the growth in the supply of gold resulting in a prolonged deflation.

In 1878 the silver interests won a major victory with passage of the Bland-Allison Act. The United States would coin silver dollars of 412.5 grains standard, the weight established by the Coinage Act of 1837, and to do so the Treasury would buy two to four million dollars of silver bullion monthly. This silver dollar, called the liberty head or Morgan dollar after its designer, George T. Morgan, was minted from 1878 until 1904, and then again in 1921.

The Silver Purchase Act of 1890 (miscalled by some strange fate the Sherman Silver Purchase Act) provided for the purchase of 4.5 million ounces monthly. Apparently this silver purchase legislation was a trade-off for passage of the McKinley tariff. Political change resulted in repeal of the Act in 1893. This, of course, was not yet the death of silver; the 1896 election, remembered probably for William Jennings Bryan's 'Cross of Gold' speech, was fought on the silver issue. Incredible gold discoveries and improved recovery methods from 1898 brought about an international gold inflation and the silver war went away as a practical matter. The current ratio varies, somewhere between 50 and 100 to 1.

A Footnote on Weights And Standards

Date	Citation	Gold $ Standard/Fine Grains		Silver $ Standard/Fine Grains		Standard	
April 2, 1792	1 Stat 246	27.0	24.75	416	371.25	Gold	11/12
						Silver	9242
Jun 28, 1834	4 Stat 699	25.8	23.2	416	371.25	Gold	9/10
Jan 18, 1837	5 Stat 136	25.8	23.22	412.5	371.25	16	9/10
Feb 21, 1853	10 Stat 160	25.8	23.22	426.67	384 (Subsid)	16.53	9/10
Feb 12, 1873	17 Stat 424	25.8	23.22	420	378 (Trade)	16.28	9/10
Feb 28, 1878	20 Stat 25	25.8	23.22	412.5	371.25 16		
Jul 14, 1890	26 Stat 289	25.8	23.22	412.5	371.25 16		
Mar 14, 1900	31 Stat 45	25.8	23.22	412.5	371.25 16		
Jan 31, 1934	Proc 2072,	15.238	13.714	412.5	371.25 27		
Mar 31 1972	86 Stat 116	12.632					
Sep 21 1973	87 Stat 352	11.368					

References for Chapter Four

Allison, W. B., *The Currency of the Future*, CCCVII North American Review 535-545 (June, 1882)

Commission on the Role of Gold in the Domestic and International Monetary Systems, *Report to the Congress*, Vols. I & II (1982). Chapter Two of Vol I is good history; see also Annex A, Vol. II, for the minority view.

Flandreau, Marc A., *Glitter of Gold: France, Bimetallism, and the Emergence of the International Gold Standard 1848-1873* (Oxford, 2003)

Hayek, Frederich A., *The Denationalisation of Money* (2d ed., IEA, 1978)

Laughlin, J. Lawrence, *The History of Bimetallism in the United States* (4th ed., 1898)

McCulloch, Hugh, and Sherman, John, et al., *Resumption of Specie Payments*, CCLIX North American Review 397-426 (Nov/Dec 1877)

Morys, Matthias, *The Emergence of the Classical Gold Standard* (Exeter Hist. Soc. Conf., 2007)

Redish, Angela, *Bimetallism: An Economic and Historical Analysis* (Cambridge, 2000)

Russell, Henry B., *International Monetary Conferences* (Harper, 1898) More than you want to know.

Sherman, John, *Recollections of Forty Years in the House, Senate and Cabinet* (1895)

CHAPTER FIVE

THE FEDERAL RESERVE ACT

The Panic of 1907 produced the Aldrich-Vreeland Act of 1908 which permitted the formation of national currency associations in each city to issue circulating notes upon deposit of national bonds, but perhaps the most important lasting contribution of the Aldrich-Vreeland Act was the creation in sections 17, 18 and 19 of the National Monetary Commission to inquire into and report . . . what changes are necessary or desirable in the monetary system of the United States.

The Aldrich-Vreeland Act and National Monetary Commission led to passage of the Federal Reserve Act which was, and remains, a creature of compromise and committee. Monetary reform started as a debate over the Aldrich Plan and, after the election of 1912, ended in consideration of the Owen-Glass Bill. Most of the furious debate centered on how many, if any, separate districts or banks should be used in the Federal Reserve System and whether the system should be run by bankers or politicians.

The Aldrich Plan really is in three iterations: Two months after the great Jekyll Island conference in November, 1910, Senator Aldrich presented to the monetary commission *A Suggested Plan for Monetary Legislation* dated January 16, 1911, and published as Sen. Doc. 784, (61st Cong., 3d Sess.); this was followed by a revised edition, again entitled *A Suggested Plan for Monetary Legislation* in October 14, 1911. The final version is a bill to incorporate the National Reserve Association of the United States which was part of the Report of the National Monetary Commission dated January 8, 1912 and published as Sen. Doc. 243, 62d Cong., 2d Sess.

This report was presented by Senator Burton on January 9, 1912 (48 Cong. Rec. 744-752) and the bill was introduced as S. 4431 by Senator Burton on January 11, 1912 (48 Cong. Rec.749). An adulatory discussion of the Glass bill (H.R. 7837, June 26, 1913) and passage of the Federal Reserve Act is thoroughly presented in H. Parker Willis, *The Federal Reserve System: Legislation, Organization, and Operation* (NY, 1923).

Two banking difficulties were addressed by the Act. First, the national problem—seasonal demand and business needs requiring an elastic currency—was to be met by Federal Reserve notes, a national currency, issued against bank collateral in the form of commercial bankers' acceptances (the real bill theory). Second, the problem of capital adequacy and ability of the banking systems to support the currency was to be met by centralization of the gold supply in reserve accounts at the Federal Reserve banks. There was no talk about abandoning the gold standard; the speeches and pamphlets of Senator Aldrich and Paul Warburg emphasize centralizing the gold supply and providing currency for trade needs on the basis of discounting commercial bills.

The title of the Federal Reserve Act says it will furnish an elastic currency, by which the framers meant a paper currency which expanded or contracted to meet the needs of trade. The United States was an exporting agricultural producer and annual flows of money were expected both across the country and internationally. Historically, and today, the Federal Reserve System had three means of affecting money in the country, but each method has changed in importance and usefulness.

First, it could set bank reserve requirements. By specifying the amount of vault cash and the size of the bank's account with the Federal Reserve, the lending of banks could be directly controlled. This is a direct method of controlling both lending and liquidity. Section 207 of the Banking Act of 1935 granted the Federal Reserve the power, by regulation, to change reserve requirements.

Second, the Fed could create bank reserves by discounting (lending against) a host of bank assets and set the discount rate; the rate it would charge banks for their loans from the Fed collateralized by eligible bank assets. This rate has, until lately, been set at 1% above the federal funds target rate.

Third, it could affect the federal funds rate by open market operations it could buy or sell government securities. A purchase of securities increased bank reserves; a sale of securities decreased bank reserves. The federal funds rate, targeted by the Fed but actually established by the banks themselves in a daily market for reserves, was the rate at which a bank short of reserves could borrow reserves from a bank with excess reserves. This rate thus was a price and cost of funds as an alternative to bank lending.

Let's look at the basis of each of these tools.

Reserve Requirements

In the original act, each commercial bank was required to maintain, by Section 19, reserves in varying percentages against its demand and time deposits. These reserves were maintained as vault cash or as deposits with the Federal Reserve Bank. The percentage requirements depending upon whether the bank was a central reserve city bank (18% of demand deposits), a reserve city bank (15%), or a country bank (12%). One half of the reserve of a bank could be in the form of its discounted paper.

Today reserve requirements have little to do with bank solvency or capital adequacy. Total bank credit is a multiple of reserves and reserves can be created or destroyed when the Federal Reserve purchases or sells securities through open market action. A bank with excess reserves can sell lend them; a bank with deficient reserves can borrow them. Reserve requirements now provide an incentive for banks to lend and a deterrent from lending too much.

Section 19, now 12 U.S.C. sec 461, permits the Federal Reserve Board to establish by regulation required reserves on most banks transactional deposits of 8% to 12%. The Monetary Control Act of 1980 establishes a low-reserve tranche, and the Garn-St. Germain Act of 1982 adds a reserve requirement exemption. This section is implemented by Regulation D, 12 CFR part 204. In January, 2009, there were total deposits in US commercial banks of $7,247 billion and required reserves of $60 billion. Not much, but actual reserves were much higher. (Source: Federal Reserve release H.8; Federal Reserve release H.3).

THE DISCOUNT RATE:

Discounting bills and notes was the primary focus of the planners of the Fed. Section 13 of the Federal Reserve Act, now 12 USC section 343, permitted a Federal reserve bank to discount "notes, drafts, and bills of exchange arising out of actual commercial transactions". While open market security purchases or sales affect banking credit generally, the discount window is open to provide loans to specific banks. Additionally, a federal reserve bank can simply lend to a member bank on its own promissory note secured by treasury securities and other things as provided in section 13 (8), 12 USC 347. This was intended to provide the elastic currency, increasing or decreasing as required by trade.

OPEN MARKET COMMITTEE PURCHASES AND SALES:

A purchase (or sale) on the open market by the Federal Reserve system has two system-wide effects. First, it creates (destroys) bank reserves because payment is credited (charged) to some bank's account at the Federal Reserve.

Second, it affects the federal funds' rate because those newly created (destroyed) reserves with the Federal Reserve affect the total demand for excess reserves traded in an interbank market to another bank which may need additional reserves. Bear in mind that by the term "reserves", we don't mean a credit balance item on the balance sheet in the usual accounting sense; reserves are vault cash and a bank's account at the Federal Reserve, which are asset items on the bank's balance sheet; the purchasing bank has a compensating liability in the form of a payable or a repurchase obligation. The purchase or sale of reserves has no effect on bank capital, only on the composition of its assets and liabilities.

There are two reasons why the Federal Reserve System may buy or sell treasury bonds in open market operations. First, bonds may be purchased specifically as an emergency measure to put additional reserves into the banking system. An example would be the 2007 crunches related to sub-prime mortgage lending. Second, and most importantly, creating or destroying bank reserves affects the federal funds rate which is a bank's alternative return to lending money. Thus buying or selling by the Federal Open Market Committee can directly affect bank lending rates and the total amount of credit offered and demanded in the economy.

Real Bills

The "real bills" theory that seasonal demand for currency could be met by discounting bills of exchange arising out of actual commercial transactions, was the intended answer to the elasticity problem. Limited as such, it was a useful adjunct to the classical gold standard to smooth out the nation's money supply which had its ups and downs depending upon America's agricultural exports. The difficulties of real bills came during the 1920s when the Fed was abusing the classical gold standard and floundering in search of a fundamental theory of the role of money. For a thorough discussion of real bills, see Richard H. Timberlake, Jr., *Gold Standards and the Real Bills Doctrine in U.S. Monetary Policy*, XI The Independent Review 325-354 (2007; Thomas M. Humphrey, *The Real Bills Doctrine*, FRB Richmond Review (October 1982); and Friedman and Schwartz.

Note on Panics

The periodic financial panics can be studied in detail. All have all been different, but all have been the same. Triggered by some event, the monetary pyramid has contracted or collapsed.

See Chapter 15 Financial Crises in Charles P. Kindleberger, *A Financial History of Western Europe*, 2d ed. (Oxford, 1993) in which he sorts outs panics in stages of speculation, euphoria, displacement and distress. For your enjoyment, look at Charles MacKay, *Extraordinary Popular Delusions and the Madness of Crowds* (1841) and Charles P. Kindleberger, *Mania, Panic, and Crashes: A History of Financial Crises* (1978). Recent publications are Robert F. Bruner and Sean D. Carr, *The Panic of 1907: Lessons learned from the Market's Perfect Storm* (Wiley, 2007) and Lawrence W. Reed, *A Lesson from the Past: The Silver Panic of 1893* (FEE, 1993). Elmus Wicker also has done several short and excellent studies of panics in the United States, including *The Banking Panics of the Great Depression* (Cambridge, 1996) and *Banking Panics of the Gilded Age* (Cambridge, 2000).

For an excellent review of the 2007 housing loan crisis, see Bordo, Michael D., *The Crisis of 2007: The Same Old Story, Only the Players Have Changed*, FRB Chicago, 10th Ann. Intl. Banking Conf., (28 Sep 2007).

Note on the Quantity Theory Of Money

The simple equation, MV = PT, states the quantity theory of money best presented by Irving Fisher. The elements are: M = money; V= velocity; P= price levels; T= transactions. It loosely but accurately describes the true rule. The difficulty, of course, is defining the money supply, measuring the price level, and determining the level of economic transactions. Velocity, the turnover rate of money (however defined) is derived and apparently has no long run stability. The Fed today struggles with these issues just as Irving Fisher did in 1912.

> You can compare Fisher's MV=PT with the Keynes' presentation of Pigou's formula n=p(k + rk) in the *Tract on Monetary Reform*. Much more on this later.

NOTE ON THE BASIS FOR ISSUANCE OF FEDERAL RESERVE NOTES

Under section 16 of the Federal Reserve Act a Federal reserve bank could discount notes, drafts, and bills of exchange arising out of actual commercial transactions; that is, notes, drafts, and bills of exchange issued or drawn for agricultural, industrial, or commercial purposes. Having acquired such commercial paper, the federal reserve bank could, under the second paragraph of Section 16, receive Federal reserve notes upon application to its Federal Reserve Agent collateralized by commercial paper. Today 12 USC 412 which embodies the bulk of Section 16. Each federal reserve bank must still collateralize its application for notes but the allowable collateral includes just about everything. The discount of commercial paper has become a minor factor. The Open Market Committee dictates the system-wide purchase of government bonds. The bonds can then be held by the Federal Reserve banks or swapped for Federal Reserve notes.

The Federal Reserve Banks were also required to keep a gold reserve against their note issue. Each Federal Reserve Bank was required, by the third paragraph of Section 16, to maintain gold reserves of forty percent against its Federal Reserve notes in actual circulation. (Paragraph 3, Section 16). Five percent of these required gold reserves were to be kept on deposit with the Treasury. (Paragraph 4, Section16). The forty percent gold reserve requirement of paragraph 3, Section 16, was reduced to 25 percent on June 12, 1945, modified to exempt deposits from reserve requirements but retained against circulating notes on March 3, 1965 (Public Law 89-3), and totally eliminated March 18, 1968 (Public Law 90-269).

Today's limitation is whatever amount can be lawfully collateralized under section 412. At December 31, 2008, outstanding Federal Reserve notes totaled $890.081 billion dollars (Federal Reserve release H.4.1).

Note on the National Monetary Commission

The work of the Commission through various scholars produced a comprehensive and valuable multi-volume study of banking in the United States and in leading European countries.

Report of the National Monetary Commission (62d Cong., 2d Sess, Sen Doc 243, Jan. 9, 1912) including proposed National Reserve Association bill

Aldrich, Nelson W., *The Work of the National Monetary Commission* (Sen. Doc. 406, 61st Cong., 2d Sess, November 29, 1909)

Aldrich, Nelson W., *Suggested Plan for Monetary Legislation* (61st Cong., 3d Sess., Sen Doc 784, 1911)

David Kinley, *The Independent Treasury of the United States and Its Relations to the Bank of the Country* (61st Cong., 2d. Sess., Sen Doc 587, 1910)

John Thom Holdsworth & Davis R. Dewey, *The First and Second Banks of the United States* (61st Cong., 2d Sess, Sen Doc 571, 1910)

A. T. Huntington and Robert J. Mawhinney, *Laws of the United States Concerning Money, Banking, and Loans*, 1778-1909 (61st Cong. 2d Sess. Sen Doc 580,1910).O.M.W. Sprague, *History of Crises under the National Banking System* (61st Cong, 2d Sess, Sen Doc 538, 1910)

Davis, Andrew McFarland, *The Origin of the National Banking System* (61st Cong., 2ds Sess, Sen Doc 582, 1910)

References for Chapter Five

Chernow, Ron, *The House of Morgan: An American Banking Dynasty and the Rise of Modern Finance* (Atlantic Monthly, 1990). Good background but no economics.

Chernow, Ron, *The Warburgs* (Random House, 1993). Good background but no economics.

Fisher, Irving, *The Purchasing Power of Money: Its Determination and Relation to Credit Interest and Crises* (1912). This is the classic.

Lamont, Thomas W., *Henry P. Davison: The Record of a Useful Life* (London, 1933).

Mints, Lloyd W., *A History of Banking Theory in Great Britain and the United States* (U. Chic. 1945)

Stephenson, Nathaniel W., *Nelson W. Aldrich* (1930)

Taus, E. R., *Central Banking Functions of the United States Treasury, 1789-1941* (Columbia, 1943)

Warburg, Paul M., *The Federal Reserve System: Its Origin and Growth* (MacMillan, 2 vols., 1930) See particularly the twelve articles in Part One of Volume Two.

Wicker, Elmus, *Banking Panics of the Gilded Age* (Cambridge, 2000) Excellent.

Wicker, Elmus, *The Great Debate on Banking Reform: Nelson Aldrich and the Origins of the Fed* (Ohio State, 2005) Excellent.

Wicker, Elmus, *Federal Reserve Monetary Policy, 1917-1933* (Random House, 1966)

Willis, H. Parker, *The Federal Reserve System; Legislation, Organization and Operation* (NY, 1923)

Wood, John H., *A History of Central Banking in Great Britain and the United States* (Cambridge, 2005)

CHAPTER SIX

GREAT WAR

In 1914 it was predicted that the war would be short because it would be so expensive. It was expensive but not particularly short. The belligerents suspended convertibility and taxed, borrowed, and printed (some things really don't change). By war's end the values of the nations' currencies were seriously out of line with their pre-war rates, and international finance was on a float.

There was general agreement that convertibility of the currencies into gold should be resumed and considerable thought was given on how to re-establish a workable monetary system. The Cunliffe Committee report in 1918 was an early look at the possibilities. In the United Kingdom the debate raged about whether or not to attempt resumption at the pre-war value of $4.87 (3£/17s/10.5d) or to devalue the pound to reflect current rates. Pretty obviously when the exchange rate is out of kilter, the alternatives come down to changing the rate or changing the national price levels. In the end Britain opted for a deflation and resumption of convertibility at the pre-war rates.

Will floating exchange rates equalize purchasing power in different currencies? One answer was offered by Gustav Cassel whose theory of Purchasing Power Parity is the idea that exchange rates will adjust themselves to equalize the purchasing power of each currency in its own country. The idea, as old as the hills, is a general tendency of prices and rates to equalize themselves as things, people, and money move around. It is a great theory; in practice, it is subject to so many qualifications that it simply remains a great theory. The most modern expression of purchasing power parity is The Economist's "Big Mac Index", now supplemented by the "Frappuccino Grande Index".

References for Chapter Six

Boyle, Andrew, *Montagu Norman* (Weybright & Talley, 1967)

Cassell, Gustav, *Money and Foreign Exchange after 1914* (1922)

Keynes, John Maynard, *Tract on Monetary Reform* (Macmillan, 1923) is widely reprinted and easy to read. This is absolutely excellent and contains insights relevant to monetary issues then and now.

Kindleburger, Charles P., *A Financial History of Western Europe, chapter 16: War Finance, Reparations, War Debts*, pp. 283-300 (Oxford, 2d ed. 1993)

Michael Pakko and Patricia Pollard, "*Burgernomics: A Big Mac Guide to Purchasing Power Parity*," St. Louis Federal Reserve Bank REVIEW pp. 9-27 (Nov/Dec 2003)

Skidelsky, Robert, John *Maynard Keynes—The Economist as Savior* 1920-1937, Chap. Five (Vol. 2, Penguin Press, 1992)

Strachan, Hew, *The First World War* (Vol 1, chapter 10, 2001). This is excellent. Look forward to future volumes.

CHAPTER SEVEN

GREAT CONTRACTION
AND GREAT DEPRESSION

Debate over the causes of the Great Depression continues, but there is general agreement that governments generally reacted badly to make it longer and worse. At the heart of the turmoil were issues of specie, currency, and foreign exchange. A cyclical peak in economic activity and in stock market prices was reached in 1929, but the great crash of September 29, 1929, was itself a minor cause compared to the slow contraction of credit effected by the Federal Reserve System. Three successive banking crises wracked the country in October 1930, March 1931, and March 1933.

The first Glass-Steagall Act of February 27, 1932, attempted to increase the money supply by making federal securities a basis under section 16 of the Federal Reserve Act for the issuance of Federal Reserve notes. The system did buy securities for a brief time and in a small amount; otherwise the main object seemed to be preventing gold outflows and sterilizing gold inflows. According to Friedman in August, 1929, our money stock was 10.6 times our gold stock; by August, 1931, it was 8.3 times the gold stock . . . From the cyclical peak in August 1929 to the cyclical trough in March 1933, the stock of money fell by over a third [Friedman &Schwartz, 299 & 361].

During the four months from his election in the fall of 1932 until his accession to office in March 1933, Roosevelt said nothing to quell economic concerns or to increase the money supply, and his first official act, Proclamation 2039, issued under authority of the Trading with the Enemy Act on March 6, 1933, closed all banks and suspended convertibility into gold. This was followed by an Emergency Banking Act on March 9, 1933, an extension of the bank holiday by Proclamation 2040 on March 9, and a licensed reopening of banks by Executive Order 6073 on March 10. Acting again under the Trading with the Enemy Act, Executive Order 6102 on April 5, 1933, proclaimed gold ownership to be hoarding and required the surrender of coin, bullion, and gold certificates. By section 43(b) (2) of the Agricultural Adjustment Act on May 12, 1933, the President was authorized to fix the weight of the gold dollar in grains nine tenths fine and also to fix the weight of the silver dollar in grains nine tenths fine at a definite fixed ratio in relation to the gold dollar at such amounts as he finds necessary from his investigation to stabilize domestic prices or to protect the foreign commerce against the adverse effect of depreciated foreign currencies . . .

This was followed by the Gold Reserve Act of 1934 on January 30, 1934, and Proclamation 2072 on January 31, 1934, setting weight of the gold dollar at 15 5/21 grains fine. This was not magic, simply a competitive devaluation intended to raise agricultural prices and increase the gold stock. Why was individual hoarding such a concern? Perhaps the answer is merely that the government wanted to profit from the coming devaluation. According to section 7 of the Gold Reserve Act of 1934, the difference was covered into the Treasury as a miscellaneous receipt.

From February 1933 through the spring of 1937, there was a substantial increase in the money supply and a good revival of business. The devaluation of the dollar produced gold imports almost uniformly from 1934 until after the Second World War. The Federal Reserve, however, continued its general passivity except for raising reserve requirement in the last half of 1936 in part to sterilize gold inflows. A result, probably, was a sharp contraction of the money supply in the spring of 1937 and a relapse into recession. Reserve requirements were relaxed in April 1938 and the money supply again rose. Ultimately the war produced accommodative purchases of treasury securities which, together with deficit financing and government spending, ushered in the age of inflation.

The Board of Governors of the Federal Reserve System was apparently wracked by personality issues as well as divisions about monetary theory. It has been suggested that Benjamin Strong, Governor of the FRB of New York, dominated the board until his death in 1928 and that thereafter Adolph C. Miller ran the show. The show was to accumulate and sterilize gold reserves, i.e., to not increase the money supply commensurately with gold inflows, and to rely upon the offering of real bills for discount to determine how much federal reserve currency should be issued.

Elmus Wicker sums it up:

The collapse of the banking system in March (1933) calamitously ended the first twenty years of Federal Reserve monetary policy. The bold experiment in central banking inaugurated in 1914 to relieve seasonal and emergency currency stringency came to grief over the unwillingness, not the incapacity, of the monetary authorities to preserve the solvency of a banking system already weakened by a prolonged business depression. That unwillingness was the direct result of the failure of an overwhelming majority of the Federal Reserve Board to understand how open market operations could be used to counteract recessions and depressions. Wicker (1966) 195.

So how dumb was the Fed? A long view and some historical perspective could have helped. The most famous quotation from Walter Bagehot's Lombardy Street (1873) was the statement of Jeremiah Harman, a director and former Governor of the Bank of England, in his testimony before the Bank Charter Committee in 1832. Mr. Harman described the actions of the Bank during a stringency of currency:

> We lent it by every possible means and in modes we had never adopted before; we took in stock on security, we purchased exchequer bills, we made advances on exchequer bills, we not only discounted outright, but we made advances on the deposit of bills of exchange to an immense amount, in short, by every possible means consistent with the safety of the Bank, and we were not on some occasions over-nice. Seeing the dreadful state in which the public were, we rendered every assistance in our power.

References for Chapter Seven

Bernanke, Ben S., *Money, Gold, and the Great Depression* (Willis Lecture, W&L, March 2, 2004)

Bordo, Michael D., *Gold, Fiat Money, and Price Stability*, NBER WP 10171 (Dec. 2003).

Chandler, Lester V., *Benjamin Strong: Central Banker* (Brookings, 1958)

Christiano, Lawrence, Motto, Roberto & Rostagno, Massimo, *The Great Depression and the Friedman-Schwartz Hypothesis*, ECB Working Paper 326 (March 2004). After 79 pages of hopeless math, they conclude the Fed could have done better.

Eichengreen, Barry, *Golden Fetters: The Gold Standard and the Great Depression, 1919-1939* (Oxford, 1992). Mr. Eichengreen blames the gold standard for our troubles, but the US wasn't following the classical specie-flow analysis and theory of the gold standard.

Eichengreen, Barry, and Temin, Peter, *The Gold Standard and the Great Depression*, NBER WP6060, 9 Cont. Eur. Hist. 183 (July, 2000). Literary but not serious.

Friedman, Milton, and Schwartz, Anna, *The Great Contraction 1929-1933* (1965) This is a separately published extract of Chapter Seven from the Monetary History.

Hsieh, Chang-Tai, and Romer, Christina D., *Was the Federal Reserve Constrained by the Gold Standard During the Great Depression? Evidence from the 1932 Open Market Purchase Program*, 66 Journal of Economic History 140-176 (2006)

Roberts, Priscilla, *Benjamin Strong, the Federal Reserve, and the Limits to Interwar American Nationalism*, FRB Richmond, 86/2 Econ. Quar. pp 61-98, 2000)

Sayers, R. S., *The Bank of England 1891-1944* (Cambridge, 1976, 3 vols.).

Timberlake, Richard H., *Federal Reserve Follies: What Really Started The Great Depression* (*http://blog.mises.org/archieves/timberlake.pdf*, 2005)

Timberlake, Richard H., Jr., *Gold Standards and the Real Bills Doctrine in U.S. Monetary Policy*, XI Independent Review pp. 325-354 (Winter, 2007)

Wicker, Elmus, *The Banking Panics of the Great Depression* (Cambridge, 1966)

Wicker, Elmus, *Federal Reserve Monetary Policy, 1917-1933* (Random House, 1966)

Wheelock, David C., *Monetary Policy in the Great Depression: What the Fed Did, and Why*, St. Louis Federal Reserve Bank Review (Mar-Apr 1992)

CHAPTER EIGHT

THE DOLLAR STANDARD AND THE EURO

DEVALUATIONS SLOW AND SUDDEN

At the end of World War II, the dollar was king, and Britain was broke. These two facts dominated international finance for the next twenty-five years. Then the dollar wasn't king any more, and the United States was broke too.

The Bretton Woods Agreements contemplated a world-wide return to fixed rate currency exchange. There was loose talk, but not much, about what to do in cases of 'fundamental dis-equilibrium', but, for a number of reasons, probably including national pride and dollar supremacy, and possibly a vague feeling of obligation to repay debts in currency of value, the idea of floating rates as a cure for fundamental disequilibrium was rejected. The result was devaluation by fits and starts.

The obvious big problem was the United Kingdom which had to mortgage itself to the world in order to save the empire. With optimism and lack of realism, Keynes, Hull & Friends thought that a fifty year loan from the United States to the United Kingdom in the amount of $3.75 billion would be sufficient to restore convertibility to the pound sterling and put Britain back on her feet. The result, the Financial Agreement between the Governments of the United States and the United Kingdom, was dated December 6, 1945, ratified July 15, 1946, and terminated with final repayment on December 31, 2006. In accordance with its promises, the United Kingdom resumed convertibility on July 16, 1947, and suspended convertibility on August 20, 1947. Thirty-five days of glory and it was over; the next fifteen years were spent discussing how to gracefully withdraw from the world.

The sterling rate at the end of World War II was $4.03 and Britain had enormous foreign debts, import controls, and an export policy called 'export or die'. After running through much of the $3.75 billion US loan in 1947, Britain came to the necessity of devaluing to $2.83 on September 20, 1949. The 1950s were a slow improvement in the British payments situation, but the 1960s brought again difficulties in trade and payments. Devaluation again to $2.40

on November 18, 1967, slowly brought some respite before the world changed in August, 1971.

Meanwhile the United States lived rather well; gold reserves steadily dropped from 20,663 metric tonnes in 1952 to 8,585 in 1973. By the end of the Eisenhower era it was clear that American imports and American military expenditure in Europe were causing a severe gold drain. Swaps, pools, and European agreements staved off the problem, but when the costs of the Vietnam War were added to the equation, it was clear that time was running out. In economic terms the difficulty of fixing currency exchange rates was similar to the attempt a century earlier to fix the bimetallic rate of exchange between gold and silver. Ultimately the established set rate broke, and President Nixon's suspension of convertibility on August 15, 1971, marks the formal end of the age of the dollar.

The European Community and the Euro

The collapse of the Bretton Woods system was a visible catalyst to development of the Euro although monetary cooperation in Europe has a much longer history. After a few attempts to patch up the Bretton Woods arrangements, currencies floated; at the same time, the Europeans were slowly coming to realize that a single currency in Europe, removed from the political necessities of individual countries, might actually promote trade, stability, and prosperity.

Various monetary unions have existed but the most notable was the Latin Monetary Union created by a Monetary Conference in Paris (Conference Monetaire entre la Belgique, la France, Italie et la Suisse) between Belgium, Switzerland, Italy and France resulting in a treaty signed December 23, 1865. This was followed by an International Monetary Conference (Conference Monetaire Internationale) in 1867 with twenty countries in attendance. Further conferences and treaties were held in 1878, 1881, and 1892. The most significant thing to come out of the Latin Monetary Union was standardization of a 1/5th ounce gold coin (actually 0.1867 troy ounce of fine gold) based on the 20 franc Napoleon. This coin circulated widely and interchangeably as the French Angel or Rooster, the Swiss Helvetia and the Italian Umberto.

In large part the stimulus for the Latin Monetary Union was the continuing problem of bimetallism, the ever changing ratio in the market value of gold and silver. The boom in gold production in Australia and California in the early 1850s had produced a premium on the value of silver coins; the boom in silver production in Nevada commencing in 1859 slowly reversed the situation and gold traded at a premium. When the union started the question was how to keep silver coinage in circulation; soon the issue became how to keep gold in circulation. The union formally existed into the twentieth century.

The First World War upset the world as it knew itself. Governments taxed, borrowed, and printed, and spent the next twenty years until the Second World War trying to put their financial Humpty Dumpty back together again. After the second war the better heads in Europe thought that maybe cooperation might be worth trying. The European Coal and Steel Community, founded by the Treaty of Paris (April 18, 1951) was precursor to the European Economic Community created by the Treaty of Rome (March 25, 1957). These (Belgium, Germany, France, Italy, Luxembourg and the Netherlands) were called the Inner Six; on January 4, 1960, by the Convention of Stockholm, Austria, Denmark, Norway, Portugal, Sweden, Switzerland, and Great Britain founded the European Free Trade Association (the Outer Seven).

A series of EEC commissions, committees, and reports in the 1960s dealt with coordination of monetary affairs. The *Report on the Realization by Stages of Economic and Monetary Union in the Community* prepared by Pierre Werner and published October 8, 1970, can serve as a starting point for study of the development of a single currency in Europe. The Werner group set out to determine the elements that are indispensable to the existence of a complete economic and monetary union . . . "A monetary union implies the total and irreversible convertibility of currencies, the elimination of margins of fluctuation in exchange rates, the irrevocable fixing of parity rates and the complete liberation of movements of capital. It may be accompanied by the maintenance of national monetary symbols or the establishment of a sole Community currency . . . The adoption of a sole currency would confirm the irreversibility of the venture." The upheavals of the 1970 left the Werner Report behind but reinforced the commitment of the European states to some sort of monetary integration.

The slow path to monetary union recommenced with a Resolution of the European Council in Brussels on December 5, 1978, which initiated the European Monetary System (SME) on March 13, 1979, and adopted the European Currency Unit (ECU) intended as a reserve asset and means of settlement between central banks. Realization in 1988 that not much was happening on the monetary front led the European Council to appoint a study Committee chaired by Jacques Delors then President of the European Commission.

The *Report on economic and monetary union in the European Community*, commonly called the Delors Report, was presented April 17, 1989, and led to the action of the European Council in Madrid on June 26, 1989, formally determining to forge ahead in a three stage program beginning July 1, 1990, which would radically change the character of the European Community.

Stage One envisioned an initiation of the process of creating an economic and monetary union and preparation and ratification of a new treaty. The Treaty on European Union, adopted at Maastricht in 1992, entered into force January 1, 1993, and contained the Protocol on the Statute of the European System of Central Banks and of the European Central Bank.

Stage Two commenced January 1, 1994, and was viewed as a learning and training process in which the basic organs and structure of the economic and monetary union would be set up. The key task for the European System of Central Banks was transition from coordination of independent national monetary policies to the formulation and implementation of a common monetary policy scheduled to take place in the final stage.

Stage Three was contemplated to commence with irrevocably locked exchange rates (effected January 1, 1999) and attribution to EC institutions of full monetary competence and control ending in actual creation and issuance of a single currency (January 1, 2002). The Euro/Dollar rate on January 4, 1999, was $1.1789; the Euro dropped to $0.8252 in October, 2000, and gradually rose to $1.59 July, 2008, then retreated to $1.40 on December 31, 2008.

The monetary policy of the European Central Bank has been a surprising success of restraint and targeting of inflation objectives. This apparently is due in part to institutional freedom from national governments and in part to an unequivocal commitment to stability of prices in the bank's governing documents.

Many of these historical papers can be found at *www.ecb.int/ecb/history* and at *http://ec.europa.eu/economy/finance/emu/history/documentation*.

INTERNATIONAL SETTLEMENTS AND CAPITAL ADEQUACY

A bank's capital gives an indication of the financial strength of the institution in the long run. Accounting-wise, capital is simply the excess of assets over liabilities. Bank capital figures can be found currently in Federal Reserve Release H.8, *www.federalreserve.gov/releases/h8*.

Except for the fact that goodwill is booked as capital and so much in the way of assets and liabilities is carried off balance sheet in structured investment vehicles, it would appear, over the years that, until the Panic of 2007, bank capitalization had improved. But dig deep in the annual reports of the major banks and see if you can separate the bank from its holding company.

Capital adequacy has become an international issue addressed under the leadership of the Bank for International Settlements (the BIZ Bank fur Internationalen Zahlungsausgleich) in Basel. The BIS was created in 1930 to deal with war reparations and has evolved into an international settlements instrument owned by fifty-five central banks.

Recent concerns over the ability of international banks to settle their accounts resulted in the *Report on Netting Schemes*, prepared by the Group of Experts on Payment Systems of the central banks of the Group of Ten countries of which Wayne D. Angell was Chairman (Basel, 1989), which was followed by the *Report of the Committee on Interbank Netting Schemes of the central banks of the Group of Ten countries*, of which Alexandre Lamfalussy was Chairman (Basel, February 1990), known generally as the Lamfalussy Report setting forth the Lamfalussy Standards. This grew slowly into the Basel II standards set forth in the *International Convergence of Capital Measurement and Capital Standards: A Revised Framework* (Basel, June 2004). These issues continue to be studied by the Committee on Payment and Settlement Systems of the BIS; their reports are published on the BIS website (http://www.bis.org/).

As implemented by the US regulatory agencies Basel II standards will require the biggest banks to weight their assets in eight categories of risk and divide their capital into categories of core capital elements (Tier 1) and supplementary capital elements (Tier 2). A bank's qualifying total capital base will consist of Tier 1 and not more than an equal amount of Tier 2 capital. Qualifying total capital must be at least 8% of risk-weighted assets. Capital adequacy is usually stated as a ratio of capital (a credit balance item) to assets (a debit balance item). U.S. banking authorities adopted 407 pages of Basel II regulations on November 2, 2007. The obvious problem, of course, is that the banks rate their own assets and liabilities.

See http://www.federalreserve.gov/newsevent/press/bcreg/bcreg20071102a1.pdf.

References for Chapter Eight

Benati, Luca, *U.K. Monetary Regimes and Macroeconomic Stylised Facts* (Bank of England WP 290, 2006) The success of inflation targeting.

Cairncross, Alec, and Eichengreen, Barry, *Sterling in Decline: The Devaluations of 1931 1949, and 1967* (Palgrave Macmillan, 2d ed., 2003)

Eichengreen, Barry, *The European Economy since 1945* (Princeton, 2007)

Einaudi, Luca, *Money and Politics: European Monetary Unification and the International Gold Standard (1865-1873)* (Oxford, 2001)

Gavin, Francis J., *The Gold Battles Within the Cold War: American Monetary Policy and the Defense of Europe, 1960-1963* (2002)

Issing, Otmar, et. al., *Monetary Policy in the Euro Area* (Cambridge, 2001)

Johnson, Harry G., *The Case for Flexible Exchange Rates, 1969*, Federal Reserve Bank of St. Louis Review (June, 1969)

Keran, Michael W., *An Appropriate International Currency—Gold, Dollars or SDRs?*, Federal Reserve Bank of St. Louis Review (Aug. 1972)

Meiselman, David I., *Worldwide Inflation: A Monetarist View*, Meiselman & Laffer, eds., The Phenomenon of Worldwide Inflation (AEI, 1975)

Morys, Matthias, *The emergence of the Classical Gold Standard*, 7th Conference of the European Historical Economic Society (July 1, 2007)

CHAPTER NINE

THINKING ABOUT MODERN MONEY

The Quantity Theory of Money Revisited

We do very well to remember the evaluation of Lord Keynes:

> **The Quantity Theory of Money . . . is fundamental. Its correspondence with fact is not open to question.** A Tract on Monetary Reform (1924)

The simple equation, MV (money x velocity) = PT (prices x transactions), states the quantity theory of money: that price levels are related to the money stock. The fundamental modern statement of the quantity theory is found in Irving Fisher's *The Purchasing Power of Money* (1912) although Gallatin described the idea in 1830. The elements are:

M (money) x V (velocity) equals P (price levels) x T (transactions)

Particularly during the period from 1940 through, perhaps, 1960s, the quantity of money and its effect on prices was dismissed as old-fashioned or summed up and ignored in economic modeling as something in the *ceteris paribus* bag. The remembrance and specter of times past—unmistakable and devastating inflations—brought quantity theory back to respectability.

In the public mind, interest rates are the measure of the looseness or tightness of money, but interest rates are merely the price of money, dependent on supply and demand. The quantity of money is half the inquiry not the whole story. Consequently when the central bank makes quantity of money decisions based on interest rates, it may well be completely wrong.

The inability to forecast interest rates or price levels led to research in the 1960s as to what measurable and controllable monetary quantity did correlate most closely with price levels. The publications of Milton Friedman are crucial, but many of the most commonly referred to studies are those coming from the Federal Reserve Bank of St. Louis. In August, 1968, Leonall C. Andersen and Jerry

L. Jordan published *The Monetary Base Explanation and Analytical Use*. Defining the base from its sources, mostly gold and federal reserve credit, and from demand for the monetary base, mostly bank reserves and public currency demand, they concluded the monetary base is under the direct control of the Federal Reserve System, it may be changed by monetary managers in a predictable manner, and such changes have an important influence on output, employment, and prices.

They followed this rather modest statement in November, 1968, with *Monetary and Fiscal Actions: A Test of Their Relative Importance in Economic Stabilization*. Their conclusion, again modest, was simply that finding of a strong empirical relationship between economic activity and either of the measures of monetary actions point to the conclusion that monetary actions can and should play a more prominent role in economic stabilization than they have up to now . . . Evidence found in this study suggests that the money stock is an important indicator of the total thrust of stabilization actions, both monetary and fiscal.

Andersen and Keith M. Carlson followed up in April, 1970, with *A Monetarist Model for Economic Stabilization*, in which they asserted that the general monetarist view is that the rate of monetary expansion is the main determinant of total spending, commonly measured by gross national product . . . Changes in total spending, in turn influence movements in output, employment, and the general price level. A basic premise of this analysis is that the economy is basically stable and not necessarily subject to recurring periods of sever recession and inflation. Major business cycle movements that have occurred in the post are attributed primarily to large swings in the rate of growth in the money stock.

I have quoted these bold monetarists at length to indicate their acknowledgment of the limitations of the quantity theory. The definition of money and the possibility of variation in velocity, based on changes in banking technology and practice were clearly recognized by the St. Louis monetarists. Indeed, a good bit of the criticism of monetarism has been based on the critic's characterization of monetarism as a certain and infallible formula. The Federal Reserve Bank of St. Louis Review continues to be a source of on-going discussion about monetary policy. Particularly see *Monetary Policy in Theory and Practice*, Proceedings of the Twenty-Fifth Annual Economic Policy Conference, July/August, 2001, and *Reflections on Monetary Policy 25 Years after October 1979*, Proceedings of a Special Conference, March/April, 2005.

The Federal Reserve claims to have emphasized growth rates of monetary aggregates during a three year period from October 6, 1979, to October 5, 1982, although any true commitment to the quantity theory is questionable. Although some academics write of the rise and fall of monetarism, the fundamental idea that there is a relation between money and prices is sound and well recognized. The Bank of England and the European Central Bank now recognize price stability as their prime function.

Note on the Neo-Classical Neo-Keynesian Synthesis

Everyone thinks in terms of some model of the economy. Economists prefer symbols and numbers unintelligible to those outside the priesthood, but two articles relatively free from more mathematics than you know and also widely cited are Clarida, Richard, Gali, Jordi, and Gertler, Mark, *The Science of Monetary Policy: A New Keynesian Perspective*, 37 J. Econ. Lit.1661 (December 1999), and Goodfriend, Marvin, and King, Robert, *The New Neoclassical Synthesis and the Role of Monetary Policy*, NBER Macroeconomics Annual 231-283 (1997) and also published as FRB Richmond Working Paper 98-5.

Note on the Monetary Pyramid

The monetary pyramid is a graphic representation of fractional reserve currency and banking. It is usually shown inverted with specie at the bottom and esoteric derivatives at the top. Thus it looks rather perilous as is intended. The pyramid is predicated on the idea that the liabilities of each layer constitute the reserve assets of the higher layers. Look first at the T-accounts of each layer, starting with the Treasury and specie at the bottom.

The Financial Upper Crust

Assets	*Liabilities*
Bank Deposits	Promises to Pay
Other Peoples' Promises	Capital (not much)

Banks

Assets	*Liabilities*
Bank Reserve Accounts	Deposits in Banks
Federal Reserve Notes	
Notes from Customers	
Bonds	

Federal Reserve System

Assets	*Liabilities*
Gold Certificates	Bank Reserve Accounts
Bonds	Federal Reserve Notes

Treasury

Assets	*Liabilities*
Gold	Gold Certificates

The Treasury owns the gold. It has issued its liability gold certificates—to the Fed. The Fed owns the gold certificates and bonds either purchased on the open market or deposited by banks. The Fed owes its Federal Reserve notes to their holders and its bank reserve accounts to its member banks. The banks own their reserve accounts, some Federal Reserve notes, some bonds, and notes from customers. The banks owe deposit accounts to customers. They pay these deposit accounts by honoring their customers' checks, orders to pay or by handing out Federal Reserve Notes, or by electronic checks in the form of credit card charges.

Note on Bank Directors Qualifying Equity Interest

The National Currency Act of 1863, which first authorized organization of national banks, required in section 39 that each director own one-half of one percent of its capital if capital exceeded $200,000. That requirement was changed by section 9 of the National Bank Act in 1864 to ten shares of $100 capital stock. Today, 12 USC section 72, amplified by 12 C.F.R. 7.2005, requires a director to own stock of an aggregate par value, aggregate shareholders' equity, or aggregate fair market value of $1,000. This requirement hasn't changed in over 140 years!

NOTE ON HOW BANKS TURNED INTO GLOBAL FINANCIAL SERVICES INSTITUTIONS

Sections 20 and 32 of the Banking Act of 1933 prohibited banks from affiliation with any organization engaged principally in the issue, flotation, underwriting, public sale, or distribution . . . of stocks, bonds, debentures, notes or other securities. This prohibition (along with a lot of other legislation) was commonly referred to as the Glass-Steagall Act and, over the years, has been slowly eroded as banks and their affiliates were authorized to do related financial services. See the Bank Holding Company Act of 1956 and the Bank Holding Company Act Amendments of 1970. This prohibition was finally repealed by the Gramm-Leach-Bliley Act in 1999. *Decensus avernum facile est.*

Note on Moral Hazard

Given the size of the monetary pyramid and its varied composition, the Fed is presented also with the really serious issue of "what else shall be monetized"?

Should the Fed, directly or through the banking system, buy everyone's bad debts because lenders expect to be bailed out? The issue in more delicate terms is called moral hazard; if everyone is to be bailed out, why should anyone care about the quality of their assets? If the issue is a want of circulating medium and a fiduciary currency is the answer, perhaps assignats were ahead of their time. Moral hazard is a highly contagious social disease infecting everyone who has any asset that can be pledged, sold, and monetized.

Issues about redeemable or fiduciary currency, reserve ratios, and capital standards are discussed with the ever-present but rarely articulated "nature of man" concern in the background. Economists, dismal scientists that we are, hate to deal with the indeterminate possibilities of error, greed, hubris, or simple speculation. A vague reference to moral hazard is as much as can be managed. The issue is not new. The committee who wrote the Bullion Report (1810) discussed at length the attitudes of bankers who were subject to seeing their own banknotes presented for redemption and those who could issue notes without fear of having to pay them:

So long as the paper of the Bank was convertible into specie at the will of the holder, it was enough, both for the safety of the Bank and for the public interest in what regarded its circulating medium, that the Directors attended only to the character and quality of the bills discounted as real ones and payable at fixed and short periods. They could not much exceed the proper bounds in respect of the quantity and amount of bills discounted, so as thereby to produce an excess of their paper in circulation, without quickly finding that the surplus returned upon them in demand for specie. The private interest of the Bank of to guard themselves against a continued demand of that nature, was a sufficient protection for the public against any such excess of Bank paper as would occasion a material fall in the relative value of the circulating medium. The restriction of cash payments, having rendered the same preventive policy no long necessary to the Bank, has removed that check upon its issues which was the public security against an excess. When the Bank Directors were no longer exposed to the inconvenience of a drain upon them for gold, they naturally felt that they had no such inconvenience to guard against by a more restrained system of discounts and advances . . . The suspension of cash payments has had the effect of committing into the hands of the Directors of the Bank of England, to be exercised by their sole discretion, the important charge of supplying the country with that quantity of circulating medium which is exactly proportioned to the wants and occasions of the public. In the judgment of the Committee, that is a trust which it is unreasonable to expect that the Directors of the Bank of England should ever be able to discharge.

Hugh McCulloch, Secretary of the Treasury under Lincoln, Johnson and Arthur, put the moral hazard issue much more bluntly:

———

No bank in the United States, the capital of which was a cash reality, and whose managers were not thieves or the borrowers of its money, has ever failed. All bank failures are fraudulent, either by mismanagement or deception in regard to capital, and all who are responsible for such failures are betrayers of trusts, and should be punished as criminals (McCulloch, 131-132.)

For other views, see Poole, William, *Market Bailouts and the Fed Put*, FRB St. Louis Review, 65 (March/April 2008); Bernanke, Ben S., and Gertler, Mark, Inside the Black Box: The Credit Channel of Monetary Policy Transmission (9 J. Econ. Perspectives 27-48 (Fall 1995).

CHAPTER TEN

THE FEDERAL RESERVE REVISITED

A revisit to the Federal Reserve System shows how the different monetary tools have evolved.

The Monetary Base and Measures of Money

There are several measures of money. These measures pick items off the balance sheets of the Federal Reserve and depository institutions but are not themselves balance sheet lines. Start with the Monetary Base as published by the Fed in Release H.3 which is presented in tables adjusted and not adjusted for seasonal variations and for changes in reserve requirements. The monetary base consists of (1) total reserves plus (2) required clearing balances and adjustments to compensate for float at Federal Reserve Banks plus (3) the currency component of the money stock plus (4) the difference between current vault cash and the amount applied to satisfy current reserve requirements. The direct measure of the monetary base is thus a picking from consolidated Federal Reserve liabilities. For the most part these federal reserve liabilities are held as assets by banks as assets (their cash and federal reserve reserves) and by the public (their cash in hand). The monetary base is thus a measure of money and of the potential for monetary creation. The monetary base for January, 2007, was 816 billion ($825,302,000,000); for January, 2008, 824 billion, and by January, 2009, 1,700 billion. See Federal Reserve Statistical Release H.3 (Table 1).

Historical data on the monetary base since January 1959 can be found at *http://federalreserve.gov/releases/h3/hist/h3hist1.pdf*. Money is defined narrowly and broadly by the Federal Reserve's statistical system. Table 1 of Federal Reserve Statistical Release H.6 gives the measure of AM1" defined as generally as currency outside the banking system and demand deposits and of AM2" which is M1 plus savings, time deposits, and retail money market accounts. These measures for the last half century give a fairly accurate picture of monetary growth.

The *Consolidated Statement of Condition of All Federal Reserve Banks* is presented in Federal Reserve Statistical Release H.4.1. *www.federalreserve.gov /releases/h4.1*

As of January 2, 2008, this would show:

	Assets	Liabilities	
Gold Certificates	11,037	791,684	Federal Reserve Notes
Securities	740,627	47,444	Deposits of Banks et. al.
Repo Agreements	56,750	40,909	Reverse Repo Agreements
Other	77,287	8,447	Other
TAF	40,000	37,217	Capital
Total	925,701	925,701	Total

Note that, as expected, treasury securities constituted 80% of the system's assets and its outstanding Federal Reserve notes constitute 85% of the system's liabilities. If money is not wampum, beads or gold, what sorts of transferable units of credit will qualify? The last two centuries in the United States has seen the change from coinage, to bank notes, to greenbacks and federal bank notes, to checks, and now to debit or credit cards. Until 2008 was the Fed only an intermediary for monetizing federal debt? But what a change 2008 brought!

As of December 31, 2008, Table 8 in H.4.1 would show:

	Assets	Liabilities	
Gold Certificates	11,037	853,168	Federal Reserve Notes
Securities	495,629	1,248,034	Deposits of Banks et al.
Repo Agreements	80,000	88,352	Reverse Repo Agreements
Other Loans	193,874	34,198	Other Stuff
CPFF	334,102		
Maiden Lanes	73,925		
"Other Assets"	620,057		
Misc.	7,061		
TAF	450,219	42,152	Capital
Total	2,265,904	2,265,904	Total

During the year 2008 the Fed sold treasury securities, purchased every conceivable asset allowable under the Federal Reserve Act, and created bank reserves but not too much currency. The big issue now is how and when the Fed will unwind itself.

Money (M1), calculated weekly in Release H.6 consists of (1) currency outside the US Treasury, Federal Reserve Banks, and the vaults of depository institution; (2) traveler's checks of non-bank issuers; (3) demand deposits at commercial banks (excluding those amounts held by depository institutions, the U.S. government, and foreign banks and official institutions) less cash items in the process of collection and Federal Reserve float; and (4) other checkable deposits (OCDs), consisting of negotiable order of withdrawal (NOW) and automatic transfer service (ATS) accounts at depository institutions, credit union share draft accounts, and demand deposits at thrift institutions. M1 generally then is cash in the hands of the public together with their checking accounts. For January, 2009, M1 was $1,575 billion.

Money (M2), also presented in Release H.6, includes and is broader than M1. Also included are (1) savings deposits (including money market deposit accounts); (2) small-denomination time deposits (time deposits in amounts of less than !000,000), less individual retirement account (IRA) and Keogh balances at depository institutions; and (3) balances in retail money market mutual funds, less IRA and Keogh balances at money market mutual funds. M2 generally then is cash in the hands of the public together with their checking and savings accounts of most varieties. M2 for January, 2009, was $8,243 billion. That is a lot of money!

Money (M3) does not appear to convey any additional information about economic activity that is not already embodied in M2 and has not played a role in the monetary policy process for many years. Consequently, it has been discontinued.

Historical data on the money supply, M1 and M2, since January 1959 can be found at *http://federalreserve.gov/releases/h6/HIST/h6hist1.pdf*.

Astounding Revelations! If prices have some relationship to money and money has some relationship to the central bank, the Fed is responsible for money and for prices. Economists can, and have, discussed elaborately every element of the quantity theory $MV=PT$, but even the most elegant of formulas are a little unrealistic when we consider something as simply as currency in circulation or "gold stock".

We can state with absolute certainty that currency in circulation at December 31, 2008, was $890,081,000,000 because we can read this number in Release H.4.1 of that date, but this basic figure may be of no use whatsoever outside the world of fiscal accounting. For years the government has studied where the dollars are and is at a total loss to know how much of our circulating medium is overseas or counterfeit. According to the Secretary of the Treasury in March, 2003, estimates dating back as far as 1960 indicate that half of all US currency in circulation is held abroad. Since currency can move undetected across borders, data and methods to estimate such holdings are inherently fragmentary and based on simplifying assumptions. Thus estimates of the total share of US currency held outside the United States are quite speculative. Nonetheless, the share has clearly grown over the past four decades. Today, we estimate that around sixty percent of all Federal Reserve notes in circulation, or about $370 billion of the $620 in circulation, is now held abroad. A fifty percent variance in either M or V should, you might think, have an impact even in a university economics department.

Similarly, the published figures reflect 261,498,899.316 fine troy ounces of gold valued at $11,041,058,821 as 2008. Eleven billion in gold is quite a lot, but it is a whole lot more if the gold is valued at, say, $800 per ounce instead of the official $42.2222. That little revaluation raises the gold stock to something over $260 billion. It doesn't matter a bit to the Federal Reserve, which holds only treasury certificates for the gold, but it does represent a goodly unrealized profit for the Treasury. Given the expressed consensus of government officials that it is merely "a barbarous relic", it is not clear why we keep it or what it is worth. Maybe the relic is not quite so barbarous?

With respect to goals, our Federal Reserve System operates at a disadvantage compared to the European Central Bank and the Bank of England. The Employment Act of 1946 and the Humphrey-Hawkins Act suggest that the Fed should simultaneously attain full employment and price stability. It was once taught that some level of inflation was necessary to have full employment, but it now generally recognized that employment effects are today, and inflation is forever. Nevertheless the ambiguity in our legislated monetary goals provides cover for both politicians and monetary officials to exercise discretion, i.e., flip-flop, whenever it suits them. In contrast, the ECB mandate is clear: price stability, which it has interpreted in practice as inflation under two percent. But inflation depends on who is figuring it, although, like pornography and the perspicacious judge, we know it when we see it. The foreign exchange rate and precious metal prices were, under classical analysis, measures that might cause concern over the accuracy of official price indices.

If gold is a constant and currency in circulation is unknown variable, what does the Fed have that it can control? The Fed's holdings of government bonds, and other assets, through open-market operations is the biggest single factor that can be both known and controlled. Ultimately things may not have changed much: the issue is still how much of the government's debt shall be "monetized"? There is no significant difference, other than interposition of the Fed, between greenbacks and Federal Reserve notes.

How important are these measures of money? Tobias Adrian and Hyun Song Shin suggest that aggregate balance sheets of financial institutions may be the best measure of whether money is loose or tight. See 14 NY Federal Reserve Bank: Current Issues in Economics and Finance 1-7 (Jan/Feb 2008). The old problem of measuring the size of the bubble and the weight of the pyramid remains.

Reserve Ratios

Reserve ratios indicate the ability of the bank to respond to deposit demands with liquidity without delay. These numbers are a little more difficult to ferret out. The definition of bank reserves that is, liquid assets which can be applied to meet deposit demands and required reserves has changed over the years, and the importance of reserves has dramatically decreased. This is a ratio of liquid assets (a debit balance item) to deposits (a credit balance item). We are not talking about capital surplus (a credit balance equity account).

The original section 19 of the Federal Reserve Act required country banks to maintain reserves equal to 12% of demand deposits and 5% of time deposits in the bank vault or in the Federal Reserve Bank; reserve city banks had a higher requirement. The Depository Institutions Deregulation and Monetary Control Act of 1980 redefines depository institutions, types of depository accounts, and acceptable forms of reserves, and the Garn-St. Germain Act of 1982 exempts certain deposits from reserve requirements.

The big change, however, over the years comes in the lessened requirement for reserves. Regulation D of the Federal Reserve Board exempts the first 8.5 million of net transactions accounts imposes a 3% reserve on the excess up to 45.8 million of deposits and 10% reserve for amounts in excess of 45.8 million. As a result at the end of 2006, required reserves were $41 billion against total deposits of $6.331 trillion. That's not much in the way of required reserves, but it may be justified. Reserves were initially required in the short term to provide liquidity and meet a run on the bank. An individual bank now can get practically all the cash (or credits to its account at the Fed) it needs from the Federal Reserve; system-wide, who knows?

So, what can a bank do to get cash or credits to its reserve account at the Fed? These provisions also have expanded. First, the second paragraph of the original Section 13 of the Federal Reserve Act permitted Federal Reserve banks to discount bank assets arising out of actual commercial transactions. This language is now found in 12 USC section 343 and further provisions make nearly all bank assets eligible for pledge to or purchase by a Federal Reserve Bank. A bank can meet both seasonable and unseasonable demands for credit by its customers by pledging their notes and assets to the Fed at the discount rate. Second, to meet its own minimal reserve requirements, the bank can borrow excess reserves (federal reserve bank balances) from other banks. It does so overnight and pays the federal funds rate for the reserves.

Discounts. Section 13 of the Federal Reserve Act is now codified at 12 U.S.C. sec. 342-347. The original act provided that any Federal Reserve Bank may discount notes, drafts, and bills of exchange issued or drawn for agricultural, industrial or commercial purposes . . . This was the "real bills" theory to provide seasonable financing adjunct to the gold standard. Just about every amendment to the Federal Reserve Act has expanded the type of asset which can be discounted. Today the Fed controls the entire money stock through open market sales and purchases. Discounts fell into disuse before 2007 and were done rarely at a penalty rate of one-half to one percent above the target fed funds rate, but the Panic of 2007 has revived discounting as a way to put money into specific banks and institutions rather than the system as a whole.

Open Market Operations

Section 14 of the Federal Reserve Act is now codified at 12 USC sec. 263, 353-359. Originally any Federal Reserve Bank may, under rules and regulations prescribed by the Federal Reserve Board, purchase and sell in the open market, at home or abroad, either from or to domestic or foreign banks, firms, corporations, or individuals, cable transfers and bankers' acceptances and bills of exchange of the kinds and maturities by this Act made eligible for rediscount, with or without the endorsement of a member bank. The two big changes are that open market operations are conducted on behalf of the whole federal reserve system and that government bonds are now eligible for purchase. This means that the Fed can supply or soak up bank reserves simply by open market purchase or sale of government securities. This is the Fed's primary means of affecting the money supply and the interest rate. See *http://www.newyorkfed.org/markets*.

The Panic Of 2007

Several provisions of the law dating from the Great Depression have been used extensively to provide liquidity. These are Section 10(b), codified as 12 USC 347b, originally added by the first Glass-Steagall Act of February 27, 1932, Section 13(3), codified as 12 USC 343, originally added by the Emergency Relief and Construction Act of July 21, 1932, and Section 13(13), codified as 12 USC 347c, added by section 403 of the Act to Provide Relief in the Existing National Emergency in Banking (1933).

Under Section 10(b) the Fed may make advances and loans to individual banks for up to four months on a basis secured to the satisfaction of the Federal Reserve Bank. This authority has been used only on a limited basis but has been revived to provide for the term auction facility. 12 CFR sec 201.4 (e) (REG A), December 12, 2007. Under Section 13(3) the Fed may extend credit in unusual and exigent circumstances to any individual, partnership, or corporation on bills secured to the satisfaction of the Federal Reserve Bank. These sections have been used to create several funding programs which indicate both the power and intention of the Fed to monetize the leaves on the trees if necessary to support the great financial pyramid. The Emergency Economic Stabilization Act will provide a wide range of Treasury purchases of assets and stock.

Term Auction Facility (TAF) December 12, 2007
Term Securities Lending Facility (TSLF) March 11, 2008
Primary Dealer Credit Facility (PDCF) March 16, 2008
ABCP MMMF Liquidity Facility (AMLF) September 22, 2008
Commercial Paper Funding Facility (CPFF) October 7, 2008)
Money Market Investor Funding Facility (MMIFF) October 21, 2008
Term Asset-Backed Securities Loan Facility (TALF) November 25, 2008
For details look at the fed websites, *http://www.financialstability.gov* and *http:// www.federalreserve.gov/monetarypolicy/bst.htm.*

Mr. Taylor and His Rule As Well As Some Others

If MV does in fact equal PT and if V is stable, then a change in the money supply (M) will produce a change in either P or T. It seems to be acknowledged that changes in M only affect T in the short run; the real effect of a change in M is a change in P with perhaps as much as two year lag. In the 1980s, V varied, probably due to financial technology, and the proper measure of M became uncertain, possibly due to the beginnings of the credit card phenomenon, although there is no definitive research on this point. Because V varied and so many measures of M were available, the MV=PT formula broke down.

So was there anything else that indicated whether money was loose or tight? An alternative was increased attention to interest rates. Since an interest rate is fundamentally a price of money determined by supply and demand, including inflationary expectations, if the government could control the price of money, it could presumably affect business activity and inflationary expectations.

John B. Taylor presented in 1992 a tentative formula to suggest the federal funds rate based on inflation and GDP. His article is readable, instructive, and has to be read if you want to follow, and appropriately discount, everything written about it since 1992. See John B. Taylor, *Discretion versus policy rules in practice*, 39 Carnegie-Rochester Conference Series on Public Policy 195 (1993). Taylor's Rule is pretty simple:

$$r = p + .5y + .5(p-2) + 2$$

> r is the indicated federal funds rate
> p is the rate of inflation over the previous four quarters
> y is the GDP gap
> 2 is the assumed equilibrium real rate of interest

Thus if (p) (rate of inflation) is 2% and there is no GDP gap, the nominal federal funds rate should be 4%. If (p) is 3% and there is no GDP gap, the nominal federal funds rate should be 5.5%, mildly tighter. If (p) is 1% and there is no GDP gap, the nominal federal funds rate should be 2.5%, mildly looser.

Taylor did not suggest causality. He presented a descriptive formula indicative of a desirable federal funds market rate given an assumed real rate of interest and up-to-date accurate measures of the GDP gap and the rate of inflation. Taylor's own assessment of the formula was that it "fits the actual policy performance during the last few years remarkably well" and that "If the policy rule comes so close to describing actual Federal Reserve behavior in recent years and if FOMC members believe that such performance was good and should be replicated in the future even under a different set of circumstances, then a policy rule could prove some guide to future decisions." Mr. Greenspan apparently thought differently.

In any event Taylor modestly suggested that at least on an experimental basis his formula could be added to the list of factors considered by the FOMC. There has been tremendous writing on whether Mr. Taylor's formula is a rule. Should we, as a rule, use our discretion to follow a rule to be discretionary unless we choose to follow a rule? What a debate! The journals burn with this issue. For background to the debate, see Kydland, F., and Prescott, E., *Rules Rather than Discretion: The Inconsistency of Optimal Plans*, 85 J. Pol. Econ. 473 (1977); Barro, R., and Gordon, D., *Rules, discretion, and reputation in a model of monetary policy*, 12 J. Mon. Econ. 101 (1983); McCallum, B., *The Use of Policy Rules in Monetary Policy Analysis*, SOMC (Nov. 2002); Bernanke, B., *Constrained Discretion and Monetary Policy* (February 3, 2002); McCallum, B., *Policy-Rule Retrospective on the Greenspan Era*, SOMC (May 2006). Recall that Mr. Taylor only said that maybe the FOMC should consider his formula which pretty well fit policy decisions in a time when they were thought to be pretty good.

Bennett T. McCallum proposes a rule based on monetary aggregates. See McCallum, *Recent Developments in the Analysis of Monetary Policy Rules*, St. Louis FRB REVIEW 3-11 (Nov/Dec, 1999).

A somewhat simpler rule based solely on a steady course for the money supply is presented by Richard Timberlake: 3.65% monetary growth except in leap years when he chooses 3.66%. (Timberlake, *Monetary Policy in the United States*, p.471).

Note on Taylor Rules

Carlstrom, C. T. & Fuerst, T. S., *The Taylor Rule: A Guidepost for Monetary Policy?*, Federal Reserve Bank of Cleveland (July, 2003)

Robert Hetzel, *AThe Taylor Rule: Is It a Useful Guide to Understanding Monetary Policy?* 86/2 Federal Reserve Bank of Richmond Economic Quarterly 1 (Spring 2000)

Issing, Otmar, *In search of monetary stability: the evolution of monetary policy*, BIS Working Paper 273 (March, 2009)

Kahn, Goerge A., and Benolkin, Scott, *The Role of Money in Monetary Policy: Why Do the Fed and ECB See It So Differently?* 92 Kansas City Fed Review (QIII) 2007, pp. 5-36.

Sharon Kozicki, *AHow Useful Are Taylor Rules for Monetary Policy*, Federal Reserve Bank of Kansas City Economic Review p.5 (Second Quarter 1999)

Meltzer, Allan H., From Inflation to More Inflation, Disinflation and Low Inflation, FRBChicago, Conf. on Price Stability (November 3, 2005)

Nelson, Edward, *Friedman and Taylor on Monetary Policy Rules: A Comparison*, 90 St. Louis FRB Review 95 (Mar/Apr, 2008)

Orphanides, A., *ATaylor Rules*, Finance and Economics Discussion Series, FRB (2007)

Orphanides, A., *Historical Monetary Policy Analysis and the Taylor Rule*, 50 J. Mon. Econ. 983 (2003)

John B. Taylor, *Discretion versus policy rules in practice*, 39 Carnegie-Rochester Conference Series on Public Policy 195 (1993)

John B. Taylor, The Need to Return to a Monetary Framework, NABE Panel (January 3, 2009). See *www.johnbtaylor.com*.

John B. Taylor and John C. Williams, *A Black Swan in the Money Market*, FRBSF Working Paper 2008-04.

Note on Inflation Targeting

In its own way the monetary policy debate is epistemological. What can we know and how can we know it? In the olden days (1970s) the monetarists knew that money ultimately affected inflation and relied on measures of the money supply because they were known and controllable. As the elements of MV=PT became less discrete, more emphasis has been placed on trying to determine the price level and how to control it. It is generally agreed that there is no intermediate or long term trade off between prices and production, but the short-term Phillips curve is alive and well among politicians seeking re-election. Although both the Bank of England and the European Community Bank explicitly recognize price stability as their primary goals, the Federal Reserve Board can pepper their speeches with talk of the dual mandate prescribed by the Humphrey-Hawkins act, even though their published academic work acknowledges (1) that the dual mandate is dead, dead, dead simply because price stability is the sine qua non of long term economic performance and (2) the long-term Phillips curve is vertical. See, for example, Bernanke, B., and Mishkin, F., *Inflation Targeting: A New Framework for Monetary Policy?* NBER Working Paper 5893 (January 1997), and Bernanke, B., *A Perspective on Inflation Targeting* (March 25, 2003). When ever you see dual mandate in a speech or article, you can be sure that equivocation and discussion of rules vs. discretion follows.

Note on Price Levels

One perplexing problem in monetary economics is calculation of the price level. There are two main government price calculations. One, the CPI, is produced by the Bureau of Labor Statistics; the other, the CPE, is produced by the Bureau of Economic Analysis of the Department of Commerce. The Fed is inclined to use the CPE. But neither takes into account foreign exchange values of the dollar or the value of traditional metallic measures like gold and silver, and neither take note of the build up of foreign held near-money claims. For price level information, see the CPE at *http://www.bea.gov/* or the CPI at *www.bls.cpi.*

Note on Inflationary Expectations

Coming out of the Great Inflation it was noted that long-term interest rates didn't decline quickly; apparently people thought the easing of inflation was only temporary. There was an inflation premium built into long-term lending. This fact has now been studied to death and nearly dominates Fed policy on price levels generally. Can you fool most of the people all the time or all of the people most of the time? The idea of well-anchored expectations substitutes for well-anchored monetary and credit aggregates. If you don't think there will be inflation, there won't be inflation; unless, of course, you believe Friedman's monetary Vincentian canon that inflation is always and everywhere a monetary phenomenon.

Note on Bank Information

Periodic reports used to be collected by each agency regulating banking. The Comptroller, FED, and FDIC each had their own system. In 1978, the Financial Institutions Regulatory and Interest Rate Control Act, PL 95-630, established an interagency body, the Federal Financial Institutions Examination Council, to prescribe uniform principles, standards and forms for the federal examination of financial institution. Samples of the forms are available on its website and the actual data submitted by banking institutions is available from the National Information Center on the web at *www.ffiec.gov/nicpubweb*.

References for Chapter Ten

Board of Governors, Federal Reserve System, *The Federal Reserve System: Purposes and Functions*. Compare the 9th edition (2005) with the Fiftieth Anniversary Edition (1963). This is on the Web: The Federal Reserve System Purposes and Functions, *http://www.federalreserve.gov/pf/pf.htm*

Coombs, Charles A., *The Arena of International Finance* (Wiley, 1976). How pointless it was.

Greenspan, Alan, *The Age of Turbulence* (Penguin, 2007). Who? Me?? Responsible???

Hayek, F. A., *Denationalisation of Money* (IEA, 1976)

Kahn, George and Benolkin, Scott, *The Role of Money in Monetary Policy: Why Do the Fed and ECB See It So Differently?*, 92 Kansas City Federal Reserve Bank Review No. 3 (2007).

Meigs, A. James, *Money Matters* (Harper & Row, 1972)

Meltzer, Allan H., *From Inflation to More Inflation, Disinflation and Low Inflation* (FRB Chic. Nov. 3, 2005).

Meulendyke, Ann-Marie, *U.S. Monetary Policy and Financial Markets* (FRB New York, 1998)

Mishkin, Frederic S., *The Economics of Money, Banking, and Financial Markets* (Addison-Wesley, 8th ed., 2007)

Poole, William, *Market Bailouts and the Fed Put*, FRB St. Louis REVIEW 65 (March/April 2008).

Warburton, Clark, *Depression, Inflation, and Monetary Policy: Selected Papers, 1945-1953* (Johns Hopkins, 1966)

Taylor, John B., *The Financial Crisis and the Policy Responses: An Empirical Analysis of What Went Wrong*, (November, 2008).

Taylor, John B., *Getting Off Track: How Government Actions and Interventions Caused, Prolonged, and Worsened the Financial Crisis* (Hoover Inst., 2009)

CHAPTER ELEVEN

TODAY, TOMORROW AND THE NEXT DAY

The more things change, the more they stay the same. This primer, I hope, provides some historical perspective on current events. The Panic of 2007 may end up having as many consequences for money and banking as the Panic of 1907. But the issues are not new. A few observations are in order as of July, 2009.

First, the bubble, balloon, and pyramid. Our existing system of money and credit is incredibly leveraged, derivativized, and securitized. Whether it is portrayed as an inverted monetary pyramid or a monetary bubble, there's money, near-money, near-near money, and near-near-near money, ad infinitum. The blurring of the never certain line between an investment security and cash is being painfully clarified. The debate used to be whether federal debt should be 'monetized'. The question today is how much of the entire monetary pyramid the Fed should promise to guarantee and monetize.

It is clear that the Fed has the authority to monetize practically any sort of debt. In fact this authority was studied in detail in 2001 in a gigantic study authored by the Federal Reserve System Study Group on Alternative Instruments for System Operations and published in 2002 as Alternative Instruments for Open Market and Discount Window Operations. The occasion was the prospect of budgetary surpluses "as far as the eye can see; what could the Fed hold as assets if there were no more federal debt?

Compare the Consolidated Statement of Condition of All Federal Reserve Banks (Statistical Release H.4.1) as of January 3, 2008, with that of January 2, 2009, to see what the Fed has done to try to support the pyramid. The Fed has swollen. However the really big question is whether the Fed will retrace its steps after the crisis is averted. If the theory is counter-cyclic monetary policy, will we see the counter phase? Messrs. Bernanke and Company intellectually know that inflation is ruinous, but will they have the courage to soak up excess reserves and insist on increased lender capital even if this means nearly total dilution of existing equity holders? This issue is further clouded by the new prospect of deficits "as far as the eye can see". Richard Fisher of the Dallas Fed has characterized the financial future as catastrophic: a frightful storm brewing in the form of un-tethered government debt.

Second, the standard. We have moved from a commodity standard-gold or silver—to a fiduciary or fiat standard. There are as many dollars as the government chooses to print and they are backed by the full faith and credit of the United States. Bank lending and the Great Inverted Pyramid are piled on top of that. Do we need a national dollar now any more than in 1792? What quantity of what commodity will have stable value over a long period of time? Gold, silver, platinum, uranium, energy units? If it is constrained by nothing but its own good conscience, can we rely on the Federal Reserve to maintain the long term purchasing power of our intergalactic credits?

Whatever shall we do with our gold? We have 261,000,000 million ounces of it. Maybe we could pass out coin or redeemable gold certificates to every American. Share the wealth, why not? Gold coin is obviously available to anyone who wants it. But at what price is it desirable to hold how much of it? Government stocks of gold in Europe and the United States overhang the market making gold price levels incredibly artificial. Gold, if there were a real market, could be the inflation target, but do we want to target the price of only one metal as the sun of our economic constellation? Gold has been considered the ultimate money for many centuries past and will probably continue to be the ultimate money in the future, but this does not imply convertibility of currencies into gold at any fixed rate, the re-emergence of the classical international gold standard based on specie-flow analysis or general circulation for day-to-day transactions. It is an inconvenient commodity, a non-productive asset (unless gold bonds come into play again), and a refuge from currency inflations.

However there is no good reason why gold can not serve as alternative money for those who wish to use it in that capacity. Recall the widespread circulation of foreign coins in the first seventy-five years of the republic and the bimetallism wars about the use of gold and silver at a fixed rate; either gold or silver could have served as basis for the currency but not both at any fixed rate for any period of time. Prices of major items can be quoted or easily calculated simultaneously in dollars, euros, and gold. That is the simplicity of floating exchange rates; you can inflate any currency by any amount and the market will work out an equilibrium. Those who hold only a single currency or who borrow or lend long term in a single currency win or lose but chose to do so.

Do you want to hold gold in some quantity? You may. Simply look in the morning paper for the quote. Indeed if you want an American gold coin you can buy American Eagle gold bullion coins of one, one-half, one-quarter, or one-tenth fine troy ounces. These have been coined by the United States Mint since passage of the Gold Bullion Coin Act of 1985. (Be careful. Look at weight. A modern $5.00 gold piece is one-tenth of an ounce, not one-quarter.) Under current law, gold coins are not the currency; they are another currency just like pounds or euros. Perhaps Kipling was right: "though we had plenty of money, there was nothing our money could buy . . ."

Third, exchange rates. It naturally follows that if the dollar is not linked to gold or anything else, we have freely floating exchange rates affected by a number of factors including foreign trade, quantity of money, purchasing power parity, and expectations of inflation and fiscal stability. The market exchange rate imposes no restraint on our money supply. Although floating exchange rates used to be much debated, they are now existing fact and world trade is flourishing. Apparently forward foreign exchange markets provide importers and exporters as much certainty as fixed exchange rates for commercial transactions; at least they don't have to guess when the next devaluation is coming.

Fourth, the banks. Banks are privately owned but they do undertake a public service of intermediating money. Several points seem worthy of consideration.

First, given their critical role in our economic system, should not banks simply be banks with financial statements that their directors, stockholders, and depositors can actually read and understand? Sections 20 and 32 of the Banking Act of 1933 prohibited banks from affiliation with any organization engaged principally in the issue, flotation, underwriting, public sale, or distribution . . . of stocks, bonds, debentures, notes or other securities. This prohibition (along with a lot of other legislation) was commonly referred to as the Glass-Steagall Act and, over the years, has been slowly eroded as banks and their affiliates were authorized to do related financial services. See the Bank Holding Company Act of 1956, the Bank Holding Company Act Amendments of 1970, and the Gramm-Leach-Bliley Act in 1999. Separating banking from all other financial activity may also cure part of the pyramid problem.

Second, bank directors need some liability. The National Currency Act of 1863, which first authorized organization of national banks, required in section 39 that each director own one-half of one percent of its capital if capital exceeded $200,000. That requirement was changed by section 9 of the National Bank Act in 1864 to ten shares of $100 capital stock. Today, 12 USC section 72, amplified by 12 CFR 7.2005, requires a director to own stock of an aggregate par value, aggregate shareholders' equity, or aggregate fair market value of $1,000. Not much wonder that bank directors, having so much at risk, have paid so little attention to the affairs of their business!

Third, capital obviously is too thin. The results of accounting trickery and rating yourself under Basel II would be ludicrous if they were not so catastrophic.

Finally, quantification. How do we measure money, velocity and prices? We have seen the difficulties. Official statistics don't come close. Should price levels be determined by gold, energy, foreign exchange, or clothing from mills in Massachusetts, South Carolina, Mexico or China? Is our money specie, Federal Reserve notes, bank credit? The issues remain: What's money? and How do we count it?

ANNOTATED CHRONOLOGY

APR 1, 1707   Act for Ascertaining the Rates of Foreign Coins, 6 Anne c 30

25 JUN 1751   Act to regulate and restrain Paper Bills of Credit in His Majesty's Colonies, 1751, 24 Geo.II, c53

APR 19, 1764   Act to prevent Paper Bills of Credit, hereafter to be issued in any of His Majesty's Colonies or Plantations in America, from being declared to be legal Tender in Payments of Money, 1764, 4 Geo. III, c34

MAY 10, 1775   Second Cont. Cong. commences, Bill of Credit issuance resolved; approved by Resolution June 22, 1775

MAR 1, 1781   Congress of the Confederation commences.

OCT 19, 1781   Capitulation at Yorktown

DEC 31, 1781   Bank of North America chartered, 20 JCC 545 (May 25, 1781), 21 JCC 1187-1190

JAN 15, 1782   Robert Morris Report on Coinage, Papers of Robert Morris, E. James Ferguson, ed., vol. 4, pp. 30-38 (Univ. Pittsburg, 1973, 4 vols), also in Boyd, Papers of Thomas Jefferson, vol. 7, pp.160-168

SEP 3, 1783   Treaty of Paris signed in Paris

MAY, 1784   Jefferson's Notes on Coinage, Papers of Thomas Jefferson, Julian P. Boyd, ed., vol. 7, pp.175-185 (Princeton Univ, 1953, 40+ vols)

MAY 13, 1785   Report of Grand Committee, Propositions Respecting the Coinage of Gold, Silver, and Copper, 28 JCC 354-358

APR 8, 1786   Report of Treasury Board on Establishment of a Mint, 30 JCC 162-182

AUG 8, 1786   Resolution, Weight and Standard of Gold, Silver, and Copper Coins, 31 JCC 503-504

OCT 16, 1786   Ordinance for Establishment of a Mint, 31 JCC 876-878

JUL 21, 1788	Constitution ratified (Congress convenes March 4, 1789).
JUL 4, 1789	Duty Act, 1st Cong., Sess. 1, chap. 2, 1 Stat.24
SEP 2, 1789	Treasury Department established (Hamilton appointed SEP 11, 1789)
AUG 4, 1790	Assumption Act, 1st Cong., Sess 2, chap. 34, 1 Stat. 138
DEC 13, 1790	Hamilton's Public Credit (National Bank) Report, Papers of Alexander Hamilton, Harold C. Syrett, ed., vol. 7, pp. 305-342 (Columbia Univ. 1963, 26 vols)
JAN 28, 1791	Hamilton's Mint Report, Papers of Alexander Hamilton, Harold C. Syrett, ed., vol. 7, pp.570-607 (Columbia Univ., 1963, 26 vols)
FEB 25, 1791	First Bank of the United States Act, 1st Cong., Sess. III, ch. 10, 1 Stat. 191
APR 2, 1792	Act establishing a Mint and Regulating the Coins, 2d Cong., Sess. I, ch.16, 1 Stat. 246. Eagle shall be 247.5 gr fine gold; 270 gr. standard (11/12 or 0.91666 fine).
FEB 9, 1793	Act regulating Foreign Coins, 2d Cong., Sess. II, ch. 5, 1 Stat 300
JUN 8, 1810	Report of the Select Committee on the High Price of Bullion (UK) reprinted as an appendix to Sumner=s History of American Currency.
APR 10, 1816	Second Bank of the United States Act, 14th Cong., Sess I, ch. 44, 3 Stat. 266
JUL 10, 1832	Jackson's veto of Second Bank Extension Act
SEP 26, 1833	Sec. Roger Taney orders withdrawal of deposits from the Second Bank
JUN 28, 1834	Gold Coin Act, 23d Cong., Sess. I, ch. 95, 4 Stat 699
JUN 23, 1836	Deposits of Public Money, 24th Cong., Sess. I, ch. 115, 5 Stat. 52, (Pet Banks) on January 1, 1837
JUL 11, 1836	Specie Circular
JAN 18, 1837	Mint Act, 24th Cong, Sess. II, ch. 3, 5 Stat. 136
JUL 4, 1840	26th Cong. Sess. I, ch. 41, 5 Stat. 385 (First Independent Treasury Act)
AUG 13, 1841	Independent Treasury Repeal Act, 27th Cong., Sess. I, ch 7, 5 Stat 439
JUL 19, 1844	Bank Charter Act 1844, 7 & 8 Vict. c32
AUG 6, 1846	An Act to Provide for the Better Organization of the Treasury Act, 29 Cong., Sess. I, ch. 90, 9 Stat. 59. (Second Independent Treasury Act)
MAR 3, 1849	Double Eagle Act, 30th Cong., Sess. II, ch109, 9 Stat 397

FEB 21, 1853	Subsidiary Coinage Act, 32d Cong., Sess. II, chap. 79, 10 Stat. 160
FEB 21, 1857	Act relating to Foreign Coins, 34th Cong., Sess. III, ch. 56, 11 Stat 163
FEB 25, 1862	Act to Authorize the Issue of United States Notes (Legal Tender Act), 37th Cong. Sess. II, ch. 33, 12 Stat. 345, supplemented by Purchase of Coin Act, 37th Cong., Sess. II, ch. 45, 12 Stat. 370 (Mar 17, 1862).
FEB 25, 1863	National Currency Act, 37th Cong., Sess. III, ch. 58, 12 Stat. 665
JUN 3, 1864	National Currency Act (National Banking Act), 38th Cong., Sess. I, ch.106, 13 Stat. 99
MAR 3, 1865	Internal Revenue Amendment Act, 38th Cong., Sess. II, ch. 78, 13 Stat. 469 at 484 (Bank Note Tax Act)
MAR 3, 1865	National Currency Amendment Act, 38th Cong., Sess. II, ch. 82, 13 Stat. 498 (90% Act)
MAY 10, 1866	Overend, Gurney & Co. insolvent
MAR 18, 1869	Act to strengthen the public Credit, 41st Cong., Sess. I, chap. 1, 16 Stat 1
FEB 10, 1870	The Coinage Act, 1870, 33 & 34 Vict. c10. A sovereign is 7.988 grams, 123.274 gr., 11/12 (.91666 fine) equals 113.00 grains fine
FEB 12, 1873	Mints, Assay-office and Coinage Act, 42d Cong., Sess. III, ch 131, 17 Stat. 424. Eagle shall be 258 gr., 0.90 fine. The Crime of 73".
SEP 18, 1873	Jay Cooke & Co crisis
JUN 20, 1874	National Bank Act, 43d Cong., Sess. I, ch. 343, 18 Stat 123
JAN 14, 1875	Resumption Act of 1875, 43d Cong., Session II, ch. 15, 18 Stat. 296. effective January 1, 1879
FEB 28, 1878	Bland-Allison Silver Purchase Act, 45th Cong., Sess. II, ch.20, 20 Stat 25
MAY 3, 1878	United States Notes (Greenbacks) issue finally set at $346,681,016.
JAN 1, 1879	Resumption effective
JUL 14, 1890	Sherman Silver Purchase Act, 51st Cong., Sess. I, ch. 708, 26 Stat. 289
NOV 8, 1890	Baring Brothers & Co. crisis
NOV 1, 1893	Repeal of Sherman Silver Purchase Act, 53d Cong. Sess. I, ch. 8, 28 Stat. 4

MAR 14, 1900	Gold Standard Act, Act of March 14, 1900, ch. 41, 31 Stat. 45 ($ set at 25.8 grains .90 fine equals 23.22 grains fine. $20/oz.)
OCT 22, 1907	Knickerbocker Trust Company insolvent
MAY 30, 1908	Aldrich-Vreeland Act, 60th Cong., Sess. I, ch. 229, 35 Stat. 546
NOV 22, 1910	Jekyll Island Conference
JAN 8, 1912	Final Report, National Monetary Commission, 62d Cong., Sess II, Sen. Doc. 243
DEC 23, 1913	Federal Reserve Act, 63d Cong., Sess II, ch. 6, 38 Stat. 251
AUG 6, 1914	Currency and Bank Note Act, 1914, 4 & 5 Geo. 6, c14
AUG 8, 1914	Defense of the Realm Act, 1914, 4 & 5 Geo. 5, c 29
SEP 18, 1914	Trading with the Enemy Act, 1914, 4 & 5 Geo. 5, c 87.
OCT 6, 1917	Trading with the enemy Act of October 6, 1917, PL 65-91, ch. 106, 40 Stat. 411
AUG 15, 1918	Committee on Currency and Foreign Exchanges after the War (Cunliffe) (Cmd. 9182, 1918)
FEB 25, 1925	Committee of the Currency and Bank of England Note Issues (Chamberlain-Bradbury Committee)
MAY 13, 1925	Gold Standard Act, 1925, 15 & 16 Geo. 5 ch. 29 (UK) ($4.867 or 3 pounds, 17 s. & 10.5d. in 1870 fineness (11/12))
MAY 17, 1931	Credit Anstalt insolvent
JUN 1931	Report of the Committee on Finance and Industry Cmnd 3897 (the MacMillan Report)
JUL 17, 1931	Danat Bank insolvent
SEP 21, 1931	Gold Standard (Amendment) Act, 1931
FEB 27, 1932	Glass-Steagall Act, 72d Cong. Sess. I, ch. 58, 47 Stat. 56 "First GS Act"
JUN 16, 1932	Lausanne Conference
JUL 21, 1932	Emergency Relief and Construction Act of 1932, 72d Cong, Sess. I, ch. 520, 47 Stat. 709
MAR 6, 1933	Pres. Proc. 2039, 48 Stat. 1689 (Bank Holiday 6-9 Mar 33)
MAR 9, 1933	An Act to Provide Relief in the Existing National Emergency in Banking, 73d Cong., Sess. I, ch. 1, 48 Stat.1
MAR 9, 1933	Pres. Proc. 2040, 48 Stat. 1691 (Banking Order)
APR 5, 1933	E.O. 6102 (Gold Hoarding Order)

MAY 12, 1933	National Economic Emergency Act (Title III of Agricultural Adjustment Act, PL 73-10, ch. 25, 48 Stat. 31 at 51-54)
JUN 5, 1933	Pub. Res. 73-10, 73d Cong., Sess. I, ch. 48, 48 Stat. 112 (Gold Clause Resolution)
JUN 12, 1933	World Economic Conference (London Monetary & Economic Conference)
JUN 16, 1933	Banking Act of 1933, PL 73-66, ch. 89, 48 Stat. 162 Second GS Act
AUG 28, 1933	E.O. 6260
JAN 30, 1934	Gold Reserve Act of 1934, PL 73-87, ch. 6, 48 Stat. 337
JAN 30,1934	Pres. Proc. 2072, 48 Stat. 1730 (Dollar devalued to $35. $ set at 15 5/21 grains .9 fine)
AUG 23,1935	Banking Act of 1935, 74th Cong., Sess. I, ch.614, 49 Stat. 684
AUG 27,1935	Pub. Res. 74-63, 74th Cong., Sess. I, ch. 780, 49 Stat. 938 (Legal Tender)
SEP 25, 1936	Tripartite Agreement (UK, France, U.S.)
FEB 28, 1939	Currency and Bank Notes Act, 1939, 2 & 3, Geo. 6, c.7
FEB 28, 1939	Emergency Powers (Defense) Act, 1939, 2 & 3 Geo. 6, c 62
SEP 5, 1939	Trading with the Enemy Act, 1939, 2 & 3 Geo. 6, c 89
SEP 4, 1939	Sterling devalued to $4.03. Exchange controls.
JUN 1942	Report of the Committee on Social Insurance and Allied Services (Beveridge Report) Cmnd 6404
JUL 22, 1944	Final Act, Bretton Woods Conference
JUL 31, 1945	Bretton Woods Agreements Act of 1945, PL 79-171, 59 Stat. 512
DEC 6, 1945	Financial Agreement between the Governments of the United States and the United Kingdom, Cmd. 6708, T.I.A.S. 1545, 60 Stat. 1841 ($3.75 billion loan)
DEC 27, 1945	Articles of Agreement of International Monetary Fund, T.I.A.S 1501, 60 Stat. 1401 (approved July, 1944, signed Washington, Dec. 1945)
FEB 14, 1946	Bank of England Act 1946, 9 & 10 Geo.6, c 27
JUL 15, 1946	PL 79-509, ch. 577, 60 Stat. 535 (US-UK Financial Agreement approved)
JUN 5, 1947	George C. Marshall, speech at Harvard. (The Marshall Plan)
JUL 16, 1947	UK convertibility resumed
AUG 20, 1947	UK convertibility suspended

APR 3, 1948	Economic Cooperation Act of 1948 (Title I of Foreign Assistance Act of 1948, PL 80-472, 62 Stat. 137
SEP 20, 1949	Sterling devalued to $2.8333; 11/11d, 250d per FTO
MAR 4, 1951	Joint Treasury-FRB Accord
APR 18, 1951	Treaty of Paris establishes ECSC
MAY 9, 1956	Bank Holding Company Act of 1956, PL 84-511, 70 Stat. 133
MAR 25, 1957	Treaty of Rome establishes EEC
AUG 20, 1959	Report on the Working of the Monetary System (Radcliffe Committee, UK)
JAN 4, 1960	EFTA signed at Stockholm
JUN 4, 1963	Silver Bullion Reserve Act, PL 88-36, 77 Stat 54
MAR 3, 1965	Federal Reserve Act Amendment, PL 89-3, 79 Stat 5, eliminates gold reserve.
JUL 23, 1965	Coinage Act of 1965, PL 89-81, 79 Stat 254, terminates silver coinage
JUN 24, 1967	Silver Certificate Act, PL 90-29, 81 Stat 77, suspends convertibility on June 24, 1968.
NOV 18, 1967	Sterling devalued to $2.40
MAR 18, 1968	Reserve Elimination Act for Federal Reserve Notes, PL 90-269, 82 Stat 50
19 JUN 1968	Special Drawing Rights Act, PL 90-349, 82 Stat. 188
12 FEB 1969	Barre Report AMemorandum on Coordination of Economic Policies and Monetary Cooperation with the Community
8 OCT 1970	Werner Report AReport on the Establishment by Stages of Economic and Monetary Union
15 FEB 1971	Decimal Day (UK)
15 AUG 1971	Doomsday. Public Papers of the Pres, Richard Nixon 1971, No. 264, pp 886
18 DEC 1971	Smithsonian Agreement Group of Ten (General Arrangements to Borrow).
31 MAR 1972	Par Value Modification Act, 1972. (US), PL 92-268, 86 Stat. 116. $38 per FTO.
24 APR 1972	Basle Agreement (Six EC central banks agree to Snake in the Tunnel of 2.25%)
1 MAY 1972	UK joins EEC snake
23 JUN 1972	UK leaves the EEC snake; Sterling floated (53 days)
12 FEB 1973	$ devalued to $42.222.
11 MAR 1973	Joint EEC float. Floating Snake.

21 SEP 1973	Par Value Modification Act Amendment (US), PL 93-110, 87 Stat. 352, $42.222 per FTO.
31 DEC 1974	E.O. 11825 40 Fed. Reg. 1003 (Gold Transactions by U.S. Citizens)
OCT 19, 1976	Bretton Woods Amendment Act, PL 94-564, 90 Stat 2660
NOV 10, 1978	Financial Institutions Regulatory and Interest Rate Control Act of 1978, PL 95-630, 92 Stat. 3641, established FFIEC.
5 DEC 1978	Brussels Summit (EC resolution to establish EMS)
MAR 13, 1979	European Monetary System entered into force
MAR 31, 1980	Depository Institutions Deregulation and Monetary Control Act of 1980, PL 96-221, 94 Stat 132
OCT 15, 1982	Garn-St. Germain Depository Institutions Act of 1982, PL 97-320
SEP 9, 1985	Single European Act (eff. 1 JUL 87)
SEP 22, 1985	Plaza Agreement
DEC 17, 1985	Gold Bullion Coin Act of 1985, PL 99-185, 99 Stat. 1179.
FEB 22, 1986	Louvre Agreement
APR 17, 1989	Report of the Committee on Economic and Monetary Union (Delors)
JUN 26, 1989	Madrid European Council (decides to launch EMU July 1, 1990)
AUG 9, 1889	Financial Institutions Reform, Recovery, and Enforcement Act of 1989, PL 101-73, 103 Stat.183
1 JUL, 1990	Stage One, EMU
5 OCT 1990	UK joins ERM 2.95 DM per L
7 FEB 1992	Treaty on European Union at Maastricht (eff.1 NOV 93)
16 SEP 1992	Black Wednesday: UK leaves the ERM At least this lasted longer than resumption of convertibility in 1947.
1 JAN 1994	Stage Two, EMU
SEP 23, 1994	Riegle Community Development and Regulatory Improvement Act Of 1994, PL 103-325, 108 Stat 2160, Section 602 Technical Amendments to Federal banking law.
DEC 15, 1995	Madrid Council
APR 23, 1998	Bank of England Act 1998, 46-47 Eliz. II, c. 11.
JUN 1, 1998	ECB established at Frankfurt am Main
JAN 1, 1999	Stage Three, EMU, Euro introduced as Unit of Account
JAN 4, 1999	Euro/Dollar rate: 1.1789

NOV 12, 1999	Gramm-Leach-Bliley Financial Services Modernization Act, Pub. L. 106-102, 113 Stat. 1338
26 OCT 2000	Euro/Dollar rate: 0.8252
1 JAN 2002	Euro currency introduced. Euro/Dollar rate:
28 DEC 2004	Euro/Dollar rate: 1.3633
OCT 13, 2006	Financial Services Regulatory Relief Act of 2006
DEC 29, 2006	Final Payment of the $3.75 billion US-UK Loan of 1946

BIBLIOGRAPHY

Basic History: The books mentioned in the introduction are fundamental.

Milton Friedman

Milton Friedman and Anna J. Schwartz, *A Monetary History of the United States, 1867-1960* (Princeton Univ. Press, 1963).

Milton Friedman and David Meiselman, "*The Relative Stability of Monetary Velocity and the Investment Multiplier in the United State, 1897-1958*" in Commission on Money and Credit, Stabilization Policies (Prentice-Hall, Inc., 1963)

Milton Friedman, *The Optimum Quantity of Money and other Essays* (Aldine Pub. Co., 1969)

Milton Friedman, *The Role of Monetary Policy*, 58 Amer. Econ. Rev. 1 (March, 1968), also published in Gibson, William E. & Kaufman, George G., *Monetary Economics* (McGraw-Hill, 1971) and as Chapter 5 of Milton Friedman, *The Optimum Quantity of Money and other Essays* (Aldine Pub. Co., 1969)

Milton Friedman, *The Quantity Theory of Money: A Restatement*, in *Studies in the Quantity Theory of Money* (Univ. Chic., 1956), also published as Chapter 2 of Milton Friedman, *The Optimum Quantity of Money and other Essays* (Aldine Pub. Co., 1969)

Milton Friedman, *Price, Income, and Monetary Changes in Three Wartime Periods*, 42 Amer. Econ. Rev. (May, 1952), also published as Chapter 8 of Milton Friedman, *The Optimum Quantity of Money and other Essays* (Aldine Pub. Co., 1969)

Milton Friedman, *The Case for Flexible Exchange Rates*, 1950, published in Milton Friedman, *Essays in Positive Economics* (Univ. Chic., 1953)

Nelson, Edward, *Milton Friedman and U.S. Monetary History, 1961-2006*, Federal Reserve Bank of St. Louis REVIEW (May/June 2007)

Modern Quantity Theory: The Best from St. Louis

Karl Brunner, *The Role of Money and Monetary Policy*, Federal Reserve Bank of
St. Louis REVIEW (July, 1968)

Leonall C. Andersen and Jerry L. Jordan, *The Monetary Base—Explanation
and Analytical Use*, Federal Reserve Bank of St. Louis REVIEW (Aug.
1968)

Darryl Francis, *An Approach to Monetary and Fiscal Management*, Federal
Reserve Bank of St. Louis REVIEW (Nov., 1968)

Leonall C. Andersen and Jerry L. Jordan, *Monetary and Fiscal Actions: A Test of
Their Relative Importance in Economic Stabilization* Federal Reserve Bank
of St. Louis REVIEW (Nov. 1968)

Meltzer, Allan H., *Controlling Money*, Federal Reserve Bank of St. Louis
Review (May, 1969)

Michael W. Keran, *Monetary and Fiscal Influences on Economic Activity—The
Historical Evidence*, Federal Reserve Bank of St. Louis Review (Nov.,
1969)

Leonall C. Andersen and Keith M. Carlson, "*A Monetarist Model for Economic
Stabilization*," Federal Reserve Bank of St. Louis Review (April 1970)

A. James Meigs & William Wolman, *Central Banks and the Money Supply*,
Federal Reserve Bank of St. Louis Review (Aug., 1971)

Teigen, Ronald L., & Rasche, Robert H., *Two Critiques of Monetarism*, Federal
Reserve Bank of St. Louis Review (Jan., 1972)

Symposium, *Controlling Monetary Aggregates* (Federal Reserve Bank of Boston,
June 10, 1969)

Symposium, C*ontrolling Monetary Aggregates II: The Implementation* (Federal
Reserve Bank of Boston, Sep. 1972)

Special Issue, *Reflections on Monetary Policy 25 Years After October 1979* (Federal
Reserve Bank of St. Louis REVIEW, Vol. 87, No. 2, Part 2)

Inflation Targeting: Prospects and Problems (Federal Reserve Bank of St. Louis
REVIEW, Vol. 86, No. 4, (Jul-Aug 2004)

The Rise and Fall of a Policy Rule: Monetarism at the St. Louis Fed, 1968-1986,
R. W. Hafer & David C. Wheelock, Federal Reserve Bank of St. Louis
Review, Vol. 83, No. 1, p.1 (Jan-Feb, 2001).

The Case for Flexible Exchange Rates, 1969, Harry G. Johnson, Federal Reserve
Bank of St. Louis Review, p.12 (June, 1969)

McCallum, Bennett T., *Recent Developments in the Analysis of Monetary Policy
Rules*, Federal Reserve Bank of St. Louis Review (Nov/Dec, 1999)

Jordan, Jerry L., *The Andersen-Jordan Approach after Nearly 20 Years*, FRB St.
Louis Review 5 (October, 1986)

What's on the Net

A Century of Lawmaking for a New Nation by the Library of Congress at http://memory.loc.gov/ammem/amlaw/lawhome.html presents Journals of the Continental Congress, Elliot's and Farrand's Debates, and Statutes at Large from 1789 to1875. The statutes at large are at http://memory.loc.gov/ammem/amlaws/lwsllink.html. The text of public laws of the 101st Congress (1989) to date can be found on Thomas http://thomas.loc.gov/bss and current US Code provisions at http://uscode.house.gov/. For statutes at large between 1875 and 1989, try the law school library.

The Board of Governors of the Federal Reserve System website at *http://federalreserve.gov* presents its statistical releases and historical data at http://federalreserve.gov/releases, the federal reserve act at http://federalreserve.gov/generalinfo/fract, and current speeches by fed officials at http://federalreserve.gov/boarddocs/speeches, Links at the several federal reserve banks provide a wealth of history and monetary policy studies. Specific statistical releases are:

> Factors Affecting Reserve Balances (H.4.1)
> http://federalreserve.gov/releases/h41/Current
> Aggregate Reserves of Depository Institutions and the Monetary Base (H.3) http://federalreserve.gov/releases/h3/Current
> Money Stock Measures (H.6)
> http://federalreserve.gov/releases/h6/Ccurrent
> The Federal Reserve System Purposes and Functions
> http://www.federalreserve.gov/pf/pf.htm

An alternate source of Federal Reserve Data is provided by the St. Louis Fed:

> FRASER—Federal Reserve Archival System for Economic Research
> *http://fraser.stlouisfed.org*
> FRED—Federal Reserve Economic Data
> http://reseach.stlouisfed.org/fred2
> ALFRED—Archival Federal Reserve Economic Data
> *http://alfred.stlouisfed.org*

US Mint http://usmint.gov/,
Federal Deposit Insurance Corporation (FDIC) http://fdic.gov/
Comptroller of the Currency http://occ.treas.gov/
Bank of England http:/http://www.bankofengland.co.uk/
Bank for International Settlements http://www.bis.org/

Bureau of Economic Analysis, Dept. Commerce http://www.bea.gov/

Bureau of Labor Statistics, Dept. of Labor http://www.bls.cpi/

Financial Management Service, U.S. Treasury http://fms.treas.gov/gold/current.html

The *North American Review* can be found at http://moa.cit.cornell.edu/moa/browse.html.

This collection from 1815 to 1900 is a treasure house of current articles on greenbacks, specie, and silver.

Supreme Court decisions can be found all over on the Web. Try *www.law.cornell.edu/supct/index.html*.

www.ingramcontent.com/pod-product-compliance
Lightning Source LLC
Chambersburg PA
CBHW022129170526
45157CB00004B/1805